Maurice's
TROPICAL FRUIT
Cook Book

by

Maurice de Verteuil

GREAT OUTDOORS
PUBLISHING CO.

4747 TWENTY-EIGHTH STREET NORTH   ST. PETERSBURG, FLORIDA 33714

SBN 8200-0806-0

DEDICATION

This book is dedicated to Jean Ellen Wilson, without whose skill, labor, and encouragement, this work would never have been produced.

Printed in the United States of America

Foreword

My mother flew a flag in front of her tiny and tropical house to signal that she was "at home" in the old sense of being willing to receive visitors and the flag was up and whipping spiritedly the day she died so suddenly. She was working on a cookbook that day, a book featuring tropical fruits, and her notes were to form the core of this volume.

My mother never believed that recipes should be followed slavishly but rather that each cook should put something of her own flair in the pot and on the table. I, too, feel that you should choose, add, eliminate, alter, season lavishly or honor seasoning in the breach, take shortcuts, substitute, experiment, taste, dare — and end up with a recipe that is uniquely yours.

My mother lived in a penthouse in Paris, a walk-up in London, a town house in Hamburg, a brick farmhouse in Canada, a houseboat in Florida and a cabin in Haiti — and her kitchen always seemed the same. I have traveled the world as deck officer of a freighter, became a sailor on wheels to explore the American west by van and the Australian outback by motorcycle. I have eaten elegantly and simply. I have enjoyed more hospitality than I profferred. Most recently, as a charter boat captain in the Caribbean, I have been responsible for feeding discriminating guests. My mother's heritage plus my own adventures at table — a world of culinary memories — resulted in this book.

For some of the basic recipes, such as orange marmalade, my thanks to the Florida State Extension Service. My mother had no notes on these kinds of things . . . all her notes were in her head.

Maurice

Sidney Lanier sang the sanguine song of retirees:
"The Robin laughed in the Orange Tree
Ho, windy North, a fig for thee:
While breasts are red and wings are bold.
And green trees wave us globes of gold,
Time's scythe shall reap but bliss for me
. . . Sunlight, song and the orange tree."

Photo by Joyce Whitlock

About the Author

One June day in 1930, Maurice de Verteuil was born in Paris. He has since made the world his home.

He grew up at sea and became an accomplished yachtsman and boat builder. He has built yachts for sailing, racing, and cruising, and one for chartering in the Caribbean. On his 28th birthday he raced his yacht "Adeline" to victory off the Australian coast.

An imaginative boat builder, he shuns the mundane, and if you don't watch him, he is apt to let his Gallic imagination get out of hand and build a work of art. His last creation was a 30-foot miniature yacht modeled after the legendary steam yachts of the 1900's — the kind commissioned and built for the Vanderbilts, Morgans, and Astors. While no steam yacht (it was powered by an efficient 40 horsepower outboard concealed in a well) it carried an aristocratic fleur de lis on the stack, the salon was decorated in green velvet trimmed with gold cord, and you steered the craft with one hand on a fine, well-varnished wooden wheel. And with the other hand, you sipped champagne, of course.

Maurice has many interests. He recently learned to fly and one of his ambitions is to cross the United States in a biplane with an open cockpit. He has already crossed the Australian outback (alone) on a motorcycle. (I believe he was the first person to accomplish this feat.) This is the equivalent of travelling through 5000 miles of our desert Southwest, only with no towns or paved roads to ease the journey. More recently, Maurice explored the U.S. in a Dodge van. It was a 36-day, 9000 mile look at America.

More than an imaginative dreamer, Maurice is a practical man (you have to be to build boats) who is always trying something new. In May of 1978, he took the Mensa Test and passed. Mensa American Limited is a society made up of people whose IQ puts them in the top 2% category. He is already familiar with fire at sea, has been shipwrecked, and known the shortage of food. He has eaten in the best restaurants of Paris, and eaten baked beans over a campfire in the Australian outback and enjoyed both. Next, he would like to learn acrobatic flying, try ox roasted over an open spit, and dine with Sir Edmund Hilary (please serve duck with orange sauce). While Maurice has never been employed as a cook (but often the volunteer) he comes by his culinary skills honestly. He is French and his mother was an accomplished cook. Her kitchen looked like a library with walls lined in cookbooks and cooking lore. In her final years her last book was published, a tome on Haitian cooking entitled "Tropical Cooking". Maurice adds his imagination and verve to his mother's scholarship and practical kitchen skills to produce this small book on "Cooking with Tropical Fruit". I hope you enjoy this book as much as we at Great Outdoors have enjoyed putting it together with Maurice.

Charles F. Allyn, Publisher.

FLORIDA FRUITS . . . Harbingers of Northern Summers

Many Florida fruits are the same as those grown in gardens and orchards and on farms "up north." In Florida, they, however, appear much earlier in the year.

. . . Florida grows more watermelons than any other state.

. . . Florida produces many varieties of strawberries.

. . . The first Caucasian to arrive in Florida found the Indian farmers growing a profusion of melons.

TROPICAL FRUITS THAT ARE OLD FRIENDS . . . since these Florida grown fruits are internationally familiar in fruit baskets, we'll only say a word about:

. . . Florida lemon acreage has increased

. . . Florida's coconut palms are being systematically eliminated by an irresistable virus. The coastal vista from Lauderdale south already looks grim without the familiar grace of these trees. The "bug" is working its way north and experts expect complete denudement.

. . . Florida once had a thriving commercial pineapple business but it was wiped out by a disease in the 30's. A dune like ridge that runs down the east coast just a bit inland is dubbed "Pineapple Ridge" by the cracker as this is where the "berry" once thrived.

. . . Florida's banana trees are a grace on the landscape and they produce a small and often delicious fruit, but there is no commercial production of bananas in the state.

WHAT TO DO ON ARBOR DAY.

In the old days, guavas dropped unnoticed from trees growing lush in vacant lots. On lazy Wednesday afternoons, children dripped with mango juice from eating the fruit of untended trees. Volunteer citrus trees produced wild and sour oranges or great hoary lemons. Practically everybody had a tropical plant growing by the doorstep.

Land development and the overwhelming wave of sun-seeking immigrants has changed all that in urban Florida. But the sun and the land are unchanged and the tropical exotic will prosper beside your patio as well as they ever grew by the porch in any fair and sun-drenched land — more durably if you care for them. All you new residents, plant a tropical tree and have yourself an exotic. Even you condominium dwellers can have an avocado tree in a pot on the balcony.

NOTES:

1. When canning fruits, when pickling or when making jellies or preserves, the Extension Food Specialists at the University of Florida Institute of Food and Agricultural Sciences, highly recommend that you use self-sealing jars rather than paraffin as the latter seal does not guarantee that humidity, mold or pests will not invade your product in Florida's tropical climate.

Pack products into hot, clean jars and adjust lids. Immerse jars into very hot water in canner or deep kettle. Water should cover jars at least an inch. If it does not, add boiling water, but do not pour directly over jars. Cover container with a close-fitting lid and bring water back to boil quickly. When boiling begins, begin timing and boil steadily and gently as recommended. (As a general rule, boil 20 minutes for pints and 25 minutes for quarts.) Remove jars immediately and cool overnight before checking seal and storing in the driest, darkest, coolest corner of your kitchen. There are no basements and few pantries in Florida!

2. BOUQUET GARNI In these recipes, this means an assortment of spices and seasonings contained rather than distributed throughout the base ingredients. I use a tea ball reserved for that purpose. You may use cheesecloth sewn into a bag or, lacking cheesecloth, a piece of pantyhose material tied into a bag. Some people like to pound the bag with a mallet once it has been made up to distribute taste more quickly and completely. Another idea for seasoning — pierce a whole onion with whole cloves stuck in it like a pin cushion.

THE ANATOMY OF THE ORANGE . . . or . . . How to Prepare, Dissect and Utilize the Florida Orange for Recipes in This Book

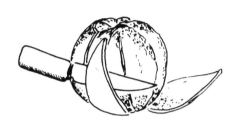

Peel it . . .

Either way . . .

Slice it . . .

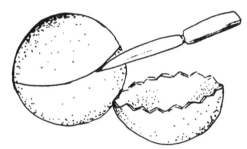

Make cups . . .

or segments

or sections

Or thaw it, undiluted . . .
(Concentrate)

Grate it . . .

THE ORANGE . . . is not native to Florida. The first of these golden apples were probably planted by Hernando de Soto who walked from Tampa to Tallahassee onward to discover the Mississippi River. Spanish bureaucracy required that each New World pilgrim carry in the pocket one hundred seeds. From such beginnings came today's Florida harvest — just short of a field box of fruit for every man, women and child in the United States.

Among the famous who have worked their own Florida orange groves are authoresses Harriet Beecher Stowe (Uncle Tom's Cabin) and Marjorie Kinnan Rawlings (The Yearling); Frederick Delius, German composer of "The Florida Suite" and "Appalachia", and Elias Openshaw, a client of Sherlock Holmes in the case of the Five Orange Pips.

In 1775, Bernard Romans wrote from British Florida that "Oranges of various kinds are worth notice as they are on many accounts useful in drink and sauces, and their leaves a good fodder for some excellent animals . . ."

In 1535, Jacques Cartier was said to have been lifted from his small boat by a large and incurious Indian who told the French explorer that "at a moon's journey along a river . . . there was a land without ice or snow, despite the fact that its inhabitants dressed in furs and continually made war . . . that oranges . . . grew there. Cartier gathered, by means of signs and tokens, that this land must be near Florida."

In 1884, a Dr. James Henshall called on a friend in Jacksonville on his way to a south Florida wilderness vacation. "Repairing to his library," the Doctor wrote, "we discussed my projected cruise over a bottle of Florida orange wine, which, by the way, equaled old Madeira in body, bouquet and flavor."

Pay no attention to the sign "Tree Ripened Fruit." That is the only way an orange will ripen—citrus must ripen on the bough or not at all. When you buy oranges, heavy is beautiful and beauty is more than skin deep. The heavier the orange, the juicer the orange and a greenish-yellow skin does not mean that that's not the most succulent orange in the bunch.

The patent for frozen orange concentrate, worth an inestimable fortune, was given freely to the people of the United States by its developers.

A medium size orange (six ounces) gives 2½ ounces of juice.

TROPICALLY BITTERSWEET ORANGE MARMALADE . . . Sophisticated on a piece of toast . . . diminutive jars make perfect hostess gifts . . . a basic ingredient for many of our recipes . . . a practical way to use those ripening oranges.

As suggested by the culinary artists at the University of Florida.

5 oranges
2 lemons

Grate fresh scrubbed oranges lightly. Cut fruits into four pieces, remove seeds, chop coarsely. Measure fruit and add 1½ times as much water. Cook slowly for 30 minutes and let stand overnight at room temperature, covered with cloth so mixture can breathe.

Water
Sugar

Measure cooked fruit and add ¾ cup sugar for each cup of orange mixture. Bring to rapid boil, guarding against scorching until candy thermometer registers 220 or until marmalade "sheets" from spoon. Remove from heat and allow to stand approximately 10 minutes or until candy thermometer registers 190.
Pour into clean, hot jars and process according to water bath method of canning explained in Note 1, page 8.
Makes approximately 5 pints.

POINTERS:

1. The sheet test: As the mixture nears the jellying point, it will drip from a spoon in separate drops. When these drops run together and "sheet" from the spoon, it is done.

2. To avoid boiling over, use heavy pot 5 times larger than the amount of mixture.

ORANGE FRUIT CUPS . . . Serve prettily in classic dessert crystal, in wine glasses or in nature's own orange rind cup!

1.   Combine fresh orange sections cut in bite size pieces with fruit cocktail and quartered marshmallows. Garnish with mint leaf.

2.   Combine the halved sections of 2 oranges, 3 bananas-sliced, ½ cup grapes-seeded and halved, 1 cup pineapple chunks (reserve ¼ cup pineapple juice), ¼ cup chopped walnuts. Add to 1 cup sweetened condensed milk beaten with 2 eggs, the ¼ cup pineapple juice and ¼ cup lime juice. Pour the milk mixture over the fruit and serve chilled.

3.   Combine the halved sections of 3 oranges, 2½ cups of pineapple chunks and ½ cup pineapple juice, the grated peel of 1 orange, ¼ cup honey, 2 T butter, ¼ cup cherries, 1 T lime juice, 2 T Triple Sec. Marinate in refrigerator for 24 hours. Two hours before serving, add 2 sliced bananas. Garnish with shredded coconut.

ORANGE SALADS . . . Ideas to start with . . . you'll want to experiment with your own combinations!

1.   On a bed of Iceberg lettuce, alternate slices of tomato and orange sections. Finish off with a dollop of orange mayonnaise topped with crushed pecans.

To make orange mayonnaise, blend 1 cup mayonnaise with 3 T orange concentrate and ½ t grated orange peel.

2.   On a bed of lettuce greens, arrange a layer of orange sections. Top this with a layer of sweet, raw onion rings scattered with fresh mushroom slices. Douse with French Orange Dressing.

To make French Orange Dressing, blend thoroughly the following ingredients: 1 6-oz. can orange concentrate, ¾ cup vegetable oil, ¼ cup wine vinegar, 3 T superfine sugar, ½ t dry mustard, ¼ t seasoned salt, 3 rotations of freshly ground black pepper, pinch of cayenne.

3. On a bed of Boston lettuce, alternate orange sections and lengthwise sliced bananas dipped in orange around a center mound of cottage cheese. Color cottage cheese with a dash of paprika and garnish bananas with chopped walnuts. Serve with boat of Orange Sour Dressing.

To make Orange Sour Dressing, blend thoroughly ½ cup each of mayonnaise, orange juice and sour cream. Add ⅛ cup honey, 1 t celery seed, 1 T capers, 1 T lime juice.

MEATS . . . prepared with an orange flair . . . Different, delicious and Floridian!

DUCK A L'ORANGE . . . Our version of the grand classic . . . when you serve it, pronounce it "A LorAnj".

Gizzards, neck, etc.
Celery tops
1 small whole onion
Water
Stock from roasting duck

Bring to boil, then simmer for 45 minutes. Add stock from roasting duck as it gathers, then chill to facilitate fat removal. Use bouillon for soup, vegetable seasoning, etc.

Duck

Roast uncovered at 325 for 25 minutes per pound without basting. If duck is very fat, prick the skin to allow fat to escape and pour it off from time to time as duck roasts. Do not pierce the skin grossly or the fat will run into the flesh. When duck has roasted as directed, remove from heat and cut into pieces and place in greased baking dish along with gizzards, etc. you have cooked separately. Cover with the following orange sauce:

Strips from 1 orange
Water
Bouillon - skim fat and strain
1 cup orange juice
1 T lime juice
1 clove garlic put through press
**3 T cornstarch made smooth in
   small quantity of water**
½ cup currant jelly

Peel strips with vegetable peeler, cover with water and boil. Drain, and boil again in enough strained bouillon to cover. Add remaining ingredients and pour mixture over duck pieces in baking dish. Bake for 45 minutes to an hour depending on whether or not you like the flesh practically falling from the bone. Garnish with fresh orange slices and orange leaves.

ORANGE CHICKEN CURRY

2 pounds of your favorite chicken
   pieces
Seasoned salt

Salt chicken and broil to brown. Place skin side up in large, heavy pot.

2 cups orange juice
2 T soy sauce
1 t curry powder
¼ t poultry seasoning
1 clove garlic, put through press

Combine these ingredients and pour over chicken in pot. Simmer until meat is just starting to be tender, some 30 - 40 minutes. Remove from heat and skim off excess fat with bulb baster.

2 large onions, coarsely chopped
2 green peppers, coarsely chopped

Add vegetables and cook until most of the liquid has evaporated and chicken is coated with a thick sauce. Onions and peppers should be crisp.

CORNISH GAME HEN TROPICAL . . . A marvelous idea for a memorable twosome picnic.

2 Cornish Game Hens
Seasoned salt
Freshly ground black pepper
2 T Olive oil

Split hens in half, season and brown lightly in olive oil in heavy skillet. Remove birds to baking pan lined with aluminum foil.

3 cloves garlic, chopped
2 T lime juice
3 bay leaves
1 6-oz can orange concentrate
½ t thyme
½ t dry mustard
1 t horseradish
1 cup chablis

Add these ingredients to skillet in which hens have been browned in order given. Bring mixture slowly to boil and simmer for 1 minute. Pour sauce over hens and bake for 40 minutes or until tender. Baste from time to time and if birds brown too soon, shield with foil. When done, remove from baking dish and chill.

SUNSHINE LAMB CHOPS

6 shoulder lamb chops
¼ cup lime juice
freshly ground black pepper
2 T vegetable oil
1 large onion, sliced

Wash chops in lime juice. Season with freshly ground pepper. Brown in hot fat. When done, remove, pour off excess fat and saute onion slices, but do not brown (lower heat).

½ cup orange juice
1 t grated orange peel
1 cup chicken broth
1 t thyme
1 teaspoon rosemary
1 t seasoned salt

Push onion slices to the side, replace chops in pan and top with sauteed onions. Combine opposite ingredients in shaker, mix well and pour half of it over chops. (Heat remaining half and serve with chops when done).

1 orange, unpeeled and sliced
   thin fresh mushrooms

Layer orange slices over chops, cover with fresh mushrooms, halved if they are large, whole if they are small. Cover and simmer for 35 - 40 minutes.

1 orange, unpeeled and sliced
   fresh parsley

Remove cooked orange slices and garnish chops with fresh slice decorated with sprig of parsley.

ORANGE STUFFING FOR ROAST CHICKEN . . . for a Florida Sunday dinner.

4 cups bread cubes - allow to dry overnight. Leftover biscuits or cornbread can be used as part of measure for a savory difference.
1 cup chopped celery
1 medium onion, chopped
1 t thyme
1 t poultry seasoning
1 t seasoned salt
1 t rosemary
freshly ground black pepper

Combine these ingredients

1 cup chicken broth
2 T butter
½ cup orange marmalade
¼ cup chopped pecans
1 T lime juice

Heat these ingredients. Pour mixture over seasoned bread cubes to moisten. Stuff bird and close cavity with a thick slice of orange. Bake according to size of chicken.

1 thick orange slice

ORANGE GLAZE HAM

Remove excess fat from pre-cooked ham. Score and stud with whole cloves. Blend 1 6-oz. can orange concentrate, ¼ cup prepared mustard, ⅓ cup dark brown sugar and brush ham generously with mixture. Bake according to ham directions, basting with additional glaze until it is finis.

BARBEQUE SPARERIBS ORANGE

Blend 1 6-oz. can orange concentrate, ¼ cup prepared mustard, ¼ cup dark brown sugar, 1 T soy sauce, 1 package onion soup mix, 2 T lime juice, 1 T sherry. Baste spareribs with mixture while broiling.

BARTRAM FILET OF FISH . . . William Bartram, British naturalist, exploring the St. Johns in 1786 made camp "to roast some trout . . . in the juice of Oranges, which, with boiled rice, afforded me a wholesome and delicious supper."

2 pounds of fish filets
seasoned salt
freshly ground black pepper
olive oil
bay leaves

Cut bay leaves in thirds with scissors and insert pieces under skin of filets. Rub the fish with oil and sprinkle with seasonings.

1 orange, sections of
1 cup orange juice
½ cup chopped green onions
1 t grated orange peel
½ t thyme
dash of freshly ground nutmeg

Combine these ingredients, spoon into shallow baking dish and lay filets thereon, skin side up, to marinate for 1 hour. Turn filets and bake at 350 for approximately 15 minutes until fish flakes, basting twice.

1 orange, thinly sliced

garnish platter with orange slices

VEGETABLES . . . piquant with orange sauce

STUFFED ORANGE SHELLS . . . with sweet potato

4 orange shells

2 cups diced, cooked sweet potatoes
¼ cup orange juice
1 T grated orange peel
¼ cup dark brown sugar
¼ cup raisins
½ stick butter
1 t cinnamon
¼ t nutmeg
¼ t allspice
¼ cup cream

Blend all ingredients. Stuff shells with mixture and place in muffin tin to insure they remain upright. Bake at 300 for 25 minutes. Remove from oven, top with marshmallow, return to oven until brown.

. . . with baked beans

4 orange shells

1 # can pork and beans
¼ cup dark brown sugar
1 T prepared mustard
2 T onion flakes
¼ cup molasses
½ jigger Triple Sec

Mix all ingredients. Stuff shells with mixture and place in muffin tin to insure they remain upright. Bake at 300 for 25 minutes.

BEETS

¾ cup orange juice
1 T cornstarch
2 t superfine sugar
½ t ginger
dash salt
1 t grated orange peel
1 T butter, melted
1 can diced beets

Combine the first 7 ingredients, bring to boil, then add beets and simmer until heated through.

CUCUMBERS

2 cucumbers, sliced
Water
1 t salt

Place cucumber slices in rapidly boiling, salted water and cook for 5 minutes. Do not overcook.

3 T butter
1 T flour
¾ cup orange juice
1 t grated orange peel
dash nutmeg
dash salt
freshly ground black pepper

Melt butter, add flour to make smooth roux, then add orange juice slowly, guarding against lumps. Add remaining ingredients, bring to boil, then simmer for three minutes. Pour over hot, drained cucumbers, stir gently and serve.

FRENCH FRIED ORANGE

1 orange, sections of

½ cup flour
½ cup beer

Mix together and allow to stand at least 2 hours for yeast to work.

Dip orange sections in batter and deep fry in vegetable oil. Drain and serve with pork.

ORANGE RICE

Cook your favorite rice, but substitute chicken bouillon for half the water.

Heat 3 T orange concentrate, add 1 t grated orange peel and add to rice when done.

ORANGE SWEET POTATO BAKE

2 lbs sweet potatoes, cooked and sliced
dark brown sugar

In greased baking dish, arrange a layer of potatoes, sprinkle with sugar. Repeat until supply is finis.

2 cups orange juice
½ cup chicken bouillon
1 t nutmeg

Blend these ingredients and pour over potato/sugar layers.

½ stick butter
1 orange, thinly sliced

Top with layer of orange slices, dotting each with butter. Bake at 350 for 45 minutes.

CARROTS

1 can sliced carrots
butter

Place drained carrots in buttered casserole

2 T Triple Sec
¼ cup brandy
⅓ cup honey
2 T lime juice
½ t freshly ground cardamon

Combine these ingredients and pour over carrots. Bake at 350 for 15 minutes or until heated through.

ORANGE TOMATO SOUP . . . a beginning for dinner that is exquisitely light and so simply different, you'll be talked about as a hostperson.

1 can condensed tomato soup
juice of 2 oranges
fresh chopped parsley

Spoon condensed soup into saucepan. Pour juice into empty can, then fill with water to make proper liquid measure. Heat slowly, stirring as needed to keep smooth. Garnish with parsley when served.

FOR LATE NIGHT SNACKS, FOR COMPANY BREAKFASTS, FOR WEEK-END BRUNCH
. . . a touch of Florida orange is a touch of class.

ORANGE FRENCH TOAST

Sliced bread, not fresh, cut in half

1 egg, well beaten
¼ cup orange juice
1 t lime juice
¼ cup superfine sugar
1 t grated orange peel
Butter

Combine all ingredients and beat well. Dip bread in mixture and fry in butter over low heat until golden brown. Wrap in foil and keep warm in oven.

½ cup orange marmalade
2 T butter, softened

Blend these ingredients. Add to pan in which toast has been fried and heat, stirring constantly.

¼ cup curacao

Add curacao and ignite, then pour over toast and serve.

OR

Dust toast with confectioners sugar, garnish with thin slice of orange and serve with honey.

ORANGE PANCAKES

To basic biscuit mix recipe, add 2 T grated orange peel and ⅓ cup chopped pecans.

ORANGE CREPES

1 egg, beaten
1 cup cream
1 cup orange juice
1 cup packaged pancake mix

Combine first three ingredients and beat. Add pancake mix and stir until most lumps are removed. Pour on to hot surface to size desired, thinning with orange juice to choice consistency.

2 sticks butter
1 cup sugar

Heat in heavy pan over low heat until caramelized (some 15 minutes), stirring with wooden spoon. Take care to avoid burning.

1 cup orange juice
2 T grated orange peel

Add to butter/sugar syrup and simmer for 3 minutes, stirring constantly.

½ cup Grand Marnier

Add liqueur, stir, and pour over crepes.

ORANGE MARMALADE BISCUITS

½ cup orange marmalade
2 T melted butter
¼ cup chopped pecans

Combine ingredients and spread in bottom of 8x8 baking pan.

2 packages refrigerated biscuits

Arrange layer of biscuits over marmalade mixture and bake at 400 for 20 minutes. Invert and turn on to plate.

ORANGE COFFEE CAKE

4 cups all-purpose sifted flour 3½ t baking powder 1 t salt ½ t baking soda	Sift these ingredients together.
1 egg 1 cup orange juice 2 T melted butter ½ cup sugar 1 t grated orange peel ½ t vanilla ½ cup oil	Blend these ingredients. Combine two mixtures and beat. Pour batter into greased, square baking pan that has been dusted with flour.
2 T flour ¼ cup dark brown sugar	Mix these two ingredients and sprinkle on batter. Bake at 400 for approximately 30 minutes.

ORANGE NUT BREAD

2¼ cups sifted flour 2 t baking powder ½ t baking soda 1 t salt 1 cup sugar	Sift these ingredients together.
1 cup chopped pecans ½ cup golden raisins 3 T grated orange peel	Add these ingredients and mix lightly with fork.
3 eggs, well beaten ½ cup cream ¼ cup orange concentrate ¾ cup butter, melted 1 t vanilla dash fresh ground nutmeg	Blend these ingredients, then add to flour mixture until flour is dampened. Bake in greased and floured loaf pan at 350 for 1 hour. When bread comes from oven, do not immediately turn out but allow to cool for ½ hour. Wrap in foil and let stand overnight before slicing as bread will crumble.
1 stick butter, softened ½ cup orange concentrate	Combine and use as spread.

ORANGE MERINGUE PIE IN CITRUS CRUST . . . A royal dessert.

1¼ cups superfine sugar 7 level T cornstarch ½ t salt	Mix these ingredients in heavy saucepan.
1½ cups hot tap water	Add water to sugar mixture a small amount at a time. Bring to boil, stirring constantly and allow to cook for some 10 minutes or until mixture is thick and clear.
3 egg yolks, beaten	Add approximately ¼ cup of the heated mixture to the egg yolks and beat in. Combine this mixture with the sugar mixture in pan, return to heat and bring to boil. Reduce heat to simmer.
1 T grated orange peel ¼ t grated lime peel	Add the grated peels and allow mixture to simmer for 5 minutes.
½ cup orange juice 2 T butter	Remove from heat, add orange juice and butter and stir in. Allow to cool.
2 cups all-purpose sifted flour ¼ t soda ¼ cup sugar 1 t salt ½ t cinnamon ¼ t ginger ¼ t cloves	Sift dry ingredients together.
⅔ cup shortening	Cut in shortening.
1 T vinegar 3 T orange juice	Mix together and then add to flour/shortening mixture, turning together lightly with fork. Chill for 1 hour, then roll out and arrange in 10" pie pan, forming a high-standing rim. Prick bottom with tines of fork and bake at 425 for 10 minutes, using foil on rim to prevent burning.
3 egg whites ¼ t cream of tartar ½ t vanilla 6 T sugar	Beat egg whites slightly. Add cream of tartar and vanilla, then beat together until stiff but not dry. Add sugar gradually and beat to stiff peaks. Spread over orange filling and bake at 350 just until golden (ten plus minutes).

ORANGE ICEBOX PIE

1 graham cracker pie shell

3 cups marshmallow bits
   (marshmallows cut in fourths
   with kitchen scissors)
1 T grated orange peel
¾ cup orange juice
2 T lime juice

Cook these ingredients together only until marshmallows are melted, stirring constantly. Chill to partial set.

1½ cups Cool Whip

Fold into marshmallow mixture, pile into pie shell and chill for 4 hours before serving.

ORANGE CHIFFON PIE FILLING

2 t unflavored gelatin
2 T cold water

Combine to soften gelatin.

4 egg yolks, well beaten
½ cup orange juice
2 T lime juice
¼ t salt
6 T sugar

Cook in top of double boiler until thick. Stir constantly and do not allow water to boil. Add softened gelatin and stir until dissolved. Chill until mixture begins to set.

4 egg whites
6 T sugar
1½ T orange peel

Beat egg whites until stiff but not dry. Add sugar and orange peel mixture gradually and beat until stiff peaks are formed. Fold into gelatin mixture, pile into crust, refrigerate until firm.

1 pint whipping cream, whipped

Garnish with dollops of whipped cream.

ORANGE PECAN PIE

3 eggs, slightly beaten
¾ cup dark syrup
½ cup orange concentrate
2 T butter, melted
1 t vanilla
½ t cardamon
⅛ t salt
1 cup sugar
½ t grated orange rind
1¼ cups pecans, whole halves

1 unbaked pie shell

Combine all ingredients in order given. Pour into pie shell and bake for 15 minutes in pre-heated 400 oven. Lower heat to 350 and bake for 45 minutes longer.

ORANGE CAKE . . . *the sunniest dessert of all!*

FROM SCRATCH ORANGE CAKE

6 T flour
1 t baking powder

Sift together.

6 eggs
6 T sugar
1 T grated orange peel

Beat eggs well. Gradually add sugar, zest of orange and finally the flour/baking powder mixture. Pour into greased and floured oblong baking pan and bake at 375 for 30 minutes or until toothpick comes out clean. Chill and cut into 3 equal pieces.

3 egg yolks
½ cup sugar
2 T cornstarch
1 cup milk
¾ cup orange juice
Confectioners sugar

Combine first 4 ingredients and cook over low heat until thick. Remove from heat and add orange juice. Cool. Thicken with confectioners sugar if necessary and spread over each layer. Arrange orange segments over icing and stack layers.

¼ cup sugar
1 T water
1 T grated orange peel
3 egg whites, stiffly beaten
dash Cointreau

Make a syrup of first three ingredients, simmering 1 minute after it comes to boil. Add to beaten egg whites gradually, beating constantly until meringue has cooled. Add Cointreau. Spread mixture over entire cake and return it to oven until meringue has browned.

ORANGE FRUIT CAKE . . . a Holiday difference!

1 cup chopped dates
½ cup walnuts, chopped
   peel of 1 orange (remove with vegetable peeler, cut in strips)

Grind these ingredients in blender.

½ cup butter, soft
1 cup sugar
2 eggs, beaten
1 t vanilla
1 t coriander seed
dash ground ginger
1 cup milk to which has been added 1 T lime juice, allow to stand for 5 minutes

Combine these ingredients with chopped fruits and nuts.

2 cups sifted flour
1 t soda
½ t salt

Sift these ingredients into above mixture. Mix well and bake in greased loaf pan at 350 for 40 minutes.

1 cup sugar
⅓ cup orange juice

Blend these ingredients and spread over cake while hot.

2 jiggers of rum

Pour over cake and ignite. When alcohol burns off, wrap in foil.

ORANGE CHEESECAKE

1 graham cracker crust

4 8-oz. packages cream cheese 1 t vanilla	Soften cheese and beat with vanilla until smooth.
2½ T flour 2½ T cornstarch 1 cup sugar	Combine dry ingredients and then add to cream cheese mixture, beating until fluffy.
6 egg yolks 1½ cups orange juice 3 T lime juice 1 T grated orange peel	Add egg yolks one at a time, then fruit ingredients, beating well after each addition.
6 egg whites	Beat until stiff, fold into cheese mixture. Pour into crust and bake at 350 for 45 minutes. Turn off oven, but allow cake to set inside cooling oven for 1 hour. Remove to rack for further cooling.
½ pint sour cream 2 T honey 1 T grated orange peel 2 cups orange sections	Combine first 3 ingredients and spread over cake. Chill. Decorate with orange sections before serving.

ORANGE BREAD PUDDING

1⅔ cup scalded milk 2 beaten eggs ½ cup sugar ¼ t salt ½ t cinnamon	Beat these ingredients together.
1 cup orange juice 1 t grated orange rind	Stir in these ingredients.
2 cups cubed stale bread ¼ cup raisins	Place bread/raisin mixture in buttered baking dish. Pour liquid mixture over cubes and stir gently to moisten. Place in pan of water and bake at 350 for 40 minutes or until knife comes out clean when inserted near edge.
1 egg ½ cup superfine sugar 1 T sherry ½ pint whipping cream, whipped	Beat egg until light, add sugar gradually, then sherry. Fold in whipped cream and chill. Serve over hot or cold pudding.

LEISURE ORANGE CAKE

Substitute orange juice for the water called for in your favorite white cake mix. Frost with fluffy white frosting. Garnish with an artistic arrangement of fresh orange segments and dust with grated coconut.

ORANGE ICING . . . for your favorite cake

2 egg yolks, beaten
3 T orange concentrate
2 T butter, melted
4 cups confectioners sugar

Beat together first four ingredients. Add sugar a little at a time and beat until smooth and creamy. Add concentrate to thin if desired.

ORANGE WHIP . . . for Angel Food Cake

4 t flour
1 cup orange juice

In small saucepan, add orange juice to flour a little at a time, stirring to make smooth.

4 egg yolks, slightly beaten
1 cup sugar
1 T grated orange peel

Add to flour mixture and cook until thick. Chill.

½ pint whipping cream, whipped

Fold into above mixture and serve on Angel Food Cake.

ORANGE DESSERT SAUCE

½ cup orange concentrate
½ cup butter
1 cup sugar
1 t lime juice
1 skimpy jigger curacao

Combine all ingredients save the last in a small saucepan. Heat to boiling point, stirring occasionally and allow to simmer for 10 minutes, covered. Remove from heat, add curacao.

ORANGE MOUSSE

1 cup whipping cream
2 T sugar
¼ t almond extract
dash allspice

Whip cream in chilled mixing bowl. Add sugar and spices.

¾ cup marshmallow bits
  (cut in fourths with
  kitchen sissors)
1 cup orange sections, diced
¾ cup orange juice
¼ cup chopped dates

Combine these ingredients and fold in whipped cream. Chill one hour before serving, garnish with almond slivers.

ORANGE MACAROONS

2 cups biscuit mix
⅓ cup sugar
⅓ cup dark brown sugar
2 T vegetable oil
2 T grated orange peel
1 T orange concentrate
3 T milk
1 egg
1 cup flaked coconut

Combine all ingredients in order given, mixing as you add. Drop dough on to greased baking sheet and bake 10 minutes at 400. Do not remove from cookie sheet at once but rather allow to stand for 5 minutes.

AN ORANGE DRINK . . . IN THE MORNING TO GET YOU STARTED, IN THE AFTERNOON TO PICK YOU UP AND AFTER FIVE TO RELAX YOU, THERE'S NOTHING LIKE IT.

ORANGE TREASURE . . . from Ft. Pierce. For a sunny brunch, chill bottle of champagne, supply of fresh orange juice. In largest and lightest goblet you own, pour ⅓ champagne, ⅓ orange juice and serve to family members as they appear, guests as they arrive.

ORANGE MILK WHIP . . . from St. Petersburg. In blender, combine ½ glass milk, ½ glass orange juice and 2 drops almond extract.

ORANGE SPICE TEA . . . from Tallahassee. Bring to boil 1 cup water, 8 whole cloves and 1 2-inch cinnamon stick and simmer covered for 5 minutes. Add ¼ cup honey, an additional cup of water and 1 cup orange juice and bring to boil once more. Remove from heat. Immerse 4 tea bags in the liquid and allow to steep for 5 minutes. Remove cover, dash with bitters and pour into cups into which you have previously placed a thin orange slice halved.

ORANGE ICI . . . from Margate. In blender, add to one 6 oz. can of orange concentrate one ice cube at a time, turning blender on and off at high speed until you obtain consistency you desire.

ORANGE EGG NOG . . . from Christmas. In blender, combine 1 pint vanilla ice cream, ⅓ cup orange concentrate and 1 egg. On low speed, add gradually 2 cups of milk. Chill and dust with freshly ground nutmeg before serving.

CAFE FLORIDA . . . from Mt. Dora. To a pot of extra strength coffee, add ¼ cup orange peel strips and 1 orange thinly sliced and keep warm for 15 minutes. Just before serving, add 1 T sugar and a dash of bitters. Top with whipped cream made from ½ pint whipping cream, 2 T sugar and 1 T grated orange peel.

CEDAR KEY SLY GROG . . . Not recommended for the timid. In blender at high speed, mix 1 fully ripe banana, 2 T lime juice, 4 cups orange juice, 3 cups rum, 3 T honey, 1 T grated lime peel, 1 t bitters until thoroughly liquified. Add 6 ice cubes and mix at low speed. Garnish chilled glass with slice of lime.

PANHANDLE PUNCH . . .mix well the following ingrediences: 1 fifth Chablis, 1 cup water, 2 cups sugar, 1 cup orange juice, 1 cup pineapple juice, ¼ cup lime juice and ¾ cup rum. Chill and serve over thin slice of orange in each large wine glass.

FLORIDA SUNRISE . . . Pour 1 part creme de cassis over cubes in large goblet. Add 4 parts tequilla, 1 part lime juice, 8 parts orange juice. Float a little grenadine over the back of a teaspoon. When green settles, stir and watch the sun rise.

ORANGE LIQUEURS . . . they're made from the orange peel and they have a thousand delicate uses. Here is a sample of suggestions and other recipes in this book call for various orange liqueurs.

TRIPLE SEC . . . use in Margaritas . . . use in apple juice and decorate the glass with a circle of lime for a brunch change from the formula Bloody Mary.

COINTREAU . . . Use a dash in a Stinger . . . use in Bananas Foster.

CURACAO . . . Make a parfait. Dissolve ½ package unflavored gelatin in small amount of hot water and allow to cool. Whip ½ pint whipping cream. When it is just shy of stiff, beat in gelatin and a skimpy jigger of curacao. Spoon into wine glasses and allow to set in refrigerator. Dust with finely chopped nuts before serving.

GRAND MARNIER . . . Combine ½ cup Grand Marnier, ¼ cup lime juice with ½ stick butter and 1 cup sugar creamed together. Pour over 2 lbs. fresh sliced peaches in buttered baking dish and bake at 350 for 30 minutes, basting occasionally.

ORANGE BUTTERS

Blend 2 T orange concentrate, 1 stick butter, ½ cup honey, squirt of lime juice and 1 t grated orange peel.   OR

Blend 2 T orange concentrate, 3 oz. package of softened cream cheese and 2 T finely chopped toasted almonds. ·OR

Combine equal amounts of orange concentrate and chunky peanut butter.

A DASH OF ORANGE . . . to enhance, to decorate, to enliven your entree. Serve alongside your main dish in your daintiest jelly dish or put one of these orange "extras" right on your meat platter.

POACHED ORANGES AU VIN

Peel of 1 orange (remove with vegetable peeler, cut in strips)
2 cups water
1 cup chablis
½ cup sugar
2 whole cloves
½ t vanilla

Combine all ingredients and cook in heavy pan over hot fire until liquid is reduced by half, about 15 minutes. Remove from heat.

2 cups orange sections

Add orange sections to hot liquid and allow to cool slightly. Arrange sections in an attractive pattern in clear serving dish and chill overnight before serving.

GLAZED ORANGE SLICES

5 thin-skinned oranges
Water to cover

Do not peel oranges, but remove ends and slice thinly. Cover oranges with water and bring to boil, then simmer until peels pierce easily with fork, approximately 1 hour. Drain.

2½ cups sugar
¼ cup water
¾ cup white vinegar
5 whole cloves
2 cinnamon sticks

Heat until sugar is dissolved, then add orange slices and cook over low heat for 90 minutes or until liquid has dissolved to form a slightly thickened sauce.

ORANGE-CRANBERRY RELISH

4 cups frozen cranberries, chopped
2 cups orange sections, diced
2 cups sugar
dash salt
¼ cup chopped walnuts
1 jigger Triple Sec

Combine all ingredients and mix well. Chill before serving.

THE GRAPEFRUIT . . . called so because it grows in clusters.

I was mate on a ship that made the sacred Mae Nan Chao Braya River when a trio of pretty Siamese girls appeared alongside in a canoe. At their feet lay a heap of fruit called "pomelo" which they threw up, one by one, the fifteen feet from the water line in return for coins. I later learned that the pomelo was the ancestor of the Florida grapefruit and I remembered that harbor transaction.

In the Caribbean, the grapefruit is often called the "Shaddock" in honor of the sea captain who first brought the pomelo from east to west.

Near the end of the last century, there was hardly a grapefruit in Florida. "They were considered a curiosity," wrote a Bradenton pioneer. Today there are 120 thousand acres of grapefruit growing in the Sunshine State and Florida produces over half the grapefruit consumed world-wide.

DIRECTIONS FOR SECTIONING FLORIDA GRAPEFRUIT: . . . (Over large bowl to preserve juice)
1. Cut slice from top of whole grapefruit.
2. With sharp knife, peel from top to bottom, cutting deep enough to remove white membrane.
3. Cut slice from bottom.
4. Cut along side of each dividing membrane from outer curve to core.
5. Remove section by section.

CAUTION — The white membrane that lies between the grapefruit peel and the fruit meat will change the taste of any recipe calling for grapefruit sections. Every vestige of this MUST BE REMOVED.

A HALF GRAPEFRUIT, CHILLED . . . the beginning of a classic breakfast.

. . . Eat it plain, dust with brown sugar or dash with Kirsch!

Why not invest in a half dozen grapefruit knives and serve one to each family member or guest along with his grapefruit? It will save you the job of cutting around sections for everyone and what's wrong with being good to yourself? In my judgment, grapefruit spoons are second best, but you may prefer them.

. . . Grapefruit is so good for you and so good to your waistline.

Impress your snowbird house guests with this mouth-watering sauce for chilled grapefruit: (You have to prepare it the night before.)

1 can tart cherries, drained
Cherry juice, preserved from above
½ cup superfine sugar
½ t cinnamon
3 T dark rum

Mint sprigs

Combine cherry juice, sugar and spice and bring to rapid boil. Cook for 5 minutes over hot fire, stirring constantly. Remove from heat and add cherries and rum. Refrigerate overnight and pour over grapefruit halves before serving. Decorate with mint.

BROILED HALF GRAPEFRUIT . . . serve as an appetizer, as a dessert or as a snack.

. . . . **DIRECTIONS FOR BROILING:** Halve grapefruit, core center with sharp knife, then cut around sections with grapefruit knife. Add topping using one of the ideas below. Place on broiler rack some 3 inches from heat and broil for approximately 15 minutes or until grapefruit is heated through.

IDEA 1 — Pour honey over grapefruit, broil. Garnish with a maraschino cherry before serving. (Prepare the night before for permeating flavor and sprinkle with rum for an extra jolt to the palate).

IDEA 2 — Sprinkle with brown sugar, add a dash of bourbon if desired and center with a cooked chicken liver.

IDEA 3 — Douse with maple syrup, sprinkle with chopped pecans.

IDEA 4 — Fill core with Drambuie, refrigerate overnight before broiling and garnish with mint before serving.

IDEA 5 — Sprinkle with cinnamon sugar, dash with fresh ground nutmeg, put a dollop of butter in the core. Garnish with citrus leaf.

IDEA 6 — Combine equal amounts of melted butter and Cointreau. Add superfine sugar to taste and stir until dissolved. Pour over grapefruit half and refrigerate overnight before broiling.

GRAPEFRUIT SECTIONS IN SALAD . . . As balmy to the taste buds as a breeze to the brow.

1. On bed of escarole, place equal amounts of grapefruit sections and cooked shrimp. Top with Grapefruit Shrimp Sauce: Blend ¾ cup mayonnaise, ½ t Tabasco, 4 T grapefruit concentrate, ¼ cup chili sauce, 1 T horseradish, 2 chopped hard boiled eggs in order given.

2. On mixed bed of Boston lettuce and escarole, arrange grapefruit sections cut to bite size, thinly sliced kumquats, pineapple chunks, banana slices sprinkled with lime juice, bite size pieces of papaya or whatever of these fruits are available. Serve with boat of Anise dressing: Blend ¼ cup salad oil, ¼ cup anise seed, freshly ground black pepper to taste, ¼ t salt, 1 T vinegar, 1 T lime juice, ½ t superfine sugar. Garnish with capers.

3. CRANGRAPEFRUIT

1 cup grapefruit juice 1 cup dark brown sugar ½ cup orange marmalade	Combine in saucepan and heat until sugar is dissolved.
2 cups cranberries 2 T fennel seed	Add and simmer until cranberry skins break (approximately 10 minutes).

4 grapefruit, sections of
   3 bananas, sliced lengthwise,
   sprinkled with lime juice
	Cool above mixture to room temperature, then add these fruits. Chill in covered container.

4. On bed of mixed green lettuces, arrange grapefruit sections, sweet onion rings and artichoke hearts. Top with Dilled Grapefruit Dressing:

1 cup grapefruit juice ¼ cup finely chopped onion 1 cup fresh dill leaves, chopped 1 t prepared mustard dash seasoned salt freshly ground black pepper	Blend these ingredients.
¾ cup grapefruit juice 4 T flour 1 cup mayonnaise 1 t paprika	Heat juice, add flour to make smooth roux. Cook slowly, but do not allow flour to brown. Remove from heat. Add mayonnaise and paprika. Combine this mixture with mixture in blender and chill.

5. GRAPEFRUIT JELLO SALAD

2 packages lime jello Grapefruit juice Water 1 pint lime sherbet, not frozen solid	Make up lime gelatin, using grapefruit juice for 1 cup water. Combine sherbet with gelatin and refrigerate.
4 cups grapefruit sections, cut to bite size ½ cup pecan pieces	When gelatin mixture begins to set, add fruit and nuts. Transfer to mold if desired. Chill to set.

Top with **CREAM MARMALADE DRESSING**

2 T water 1 T cornstarch ⅓ cup lime juice ¾ cup orange marmalade 2 eggs, beaten	Blend these ingredients, then cook until thick, stirring constantly. Cool to room temperature, then chill.
½ pint whipping cream, whipped	Just before serving, fold whipped cream into marmalade mixture.

GRAPEFRUIT SNAPPER ESCAVE'CHE

2 pounds snapper steaks, cut into strips, sprinkled with lime juice

Spray heavy skillet with Pam. Arrange snapper strips therein.

1 6-oz. can grapefruit concentrate
1 t seasoned salt
freshly ground black pepper
1 T dark brown sugar
½ t dry mustard
dash of cayenne pepper
½ cup salad oil

Blend these ingredients and heat. Pour mixture over fish and simmer for 10 to 12 minutes. Remove from heat, cover. Refrigerate overnight before serving.

BAKED PORK CHOPS WITH GRAPEFRUIT STUFFING

½ stick butter
½ cup chopped celery
1 small onion, chopped

In the butter, saute the onion and the celery, but do not allow them to brown.

2 cups bread cubes, dried
½ cup leftover rice
1 T poultry seasoning
1 t seasoned salt
freshly ground black pepper
1 small can water chestnuts, drained and chopped
2 T grated peel

Combine these ingredients and then dampen with above butter/vegetable mixture.

2 cups grapefruit sections

Add sections and stir carefully to mix. Spoon mixture into heavy baking pan that has been lightly oiled.

6 thick pork chops, trimmed of excess fat

Place chops over dressing in layer.

½ cup raisins
¼ cup sherry

Combine raisins and sherry and spoon equal amounts of mixture on to each chop. Cover and bake for approximately 1 hour.

GRAPEFRUIT SHRIMP CURRY

5 T butter
1 small onion, finely chopped

Saute onion in butter. Do not brown.

5 T flour
2 t seasoned salt
1 T curry powder
1 chicken bouillon cube

Blend in flour to make roux. Add seasonings and bouillon cube. Blend.

2½ cups milk
½ cup grapefruit juice

Add liquids. At this point, you must stir constantly and guard against curdling. Cook until thick.

2 pounds cooked shrimp, peeled
1 cup grapefruit sections, cut in half or bite size

Add shrimp and grapefruit sections and heat through over low heat. Serve on bed of rice.

AIRY GRAPEFRUIT PIE

3 cups grapefruit sections	Allow to drain well.
2 packages unflavored gelatin ¼ cup cold water	Allow gelatin to dissolve.
5 egg yolks ½ cup grapefruit juice 2 T lime juice ½ cup sugar ½ t salt	Cook in double boiler, stirring constantly, until mixture begins to thicken. Add gelatin/water mixture and allow the liquid to boil for one minute. Remove from heat and allow to cool, stirring often.
5 egg whites ½ cup sugar ½ t cream of tartar	Beat until stiff and dry and until meringue forms peaks. Fold into cooled mixture, then fold in grapefruit sections.
1 baked pie shell	Place filling in pie shell and allow pie to chill before serving.
½ pint whipping cream, whipped	Serve each piece with a dollop of whipped cream.

GRAPEFRUIT SWEET POTATO BAKE

4 cups grapefruit sections ¾ cup grapefruit juice ½ cup dark brown sugar	Combine and allow to stand for 30 minutes. Drain sections, reserving liquid.
½ t pumpkin pie spice· ½ stick butter, melted ½ t salt	Combine these ingredients and add to liquid.
4 sliced sweet potatoes, cooked and sliced	Place a layer of potatoes in bottom of buttered casserole, then cover with a layer of grapefruit sections. Alternate until all munitions are exhausted. Pour liquid over dish and bake for some 30 minutes or until heated through at 350. Remove from oven, top with Honey Meringue and return to oven to brown.
1 egg white 4 T water pinch of salt 1 cup honey ¼ t cream of tartar	Combine all ingredients and cook in double boiler, beating constantly with rotary beater. When meringue peaks, remove from heat and continue beating until creamy.

TANGERINE . . . it's a color fashion magazines are fond of, it's the name of a girl in a song, it's the lazy person's orange because the peel zips off . . . you can substitute tangerine for most recipes that call for mandarin oranges

OR you can use them for:

A TANGERINE SALAD

Add tangerine sections to your favorite tossed green salad along with salted walnuts browned in butter.

Make an entrancing slaw by mixing halved tangerine sections with an equal amount of shredded cabbage. Make interesting with shavings of green pepper and moisten with your favorite slaw dressing.

TANGERINE JUBILEE . . . many a world-traveled gourmet has never tasted this dessert.

3 cups orange juice
3 T sugar
6 tangerines, sections of
2 jiggers brandy, heated

Melt sugar in orange juice in chafing dish at the table. Add tangerine sections. Allow to heat through, then add brandy and ignite. Serve in warmed dessert dishes.

TANGERINE ICE CREAM . . . the name "tangerine" is derived from "Tangier" where the fruit made a long stop in history before it was brought to the new World. The cool-loving Moors would have loved the convenience of this recipe.

1 6oz. can frozen tangerine
**   concentrate, thawed**
½ pint whipping cream, whipped

Fold together.

2 egg whites
1 cup superfine sugar

Beat egg whites until stiff but not dry. Add sugar gradually, beating each time until whites form stiff peaks. Fold whites into concentrate/cream mixture and freeze in ice tray.

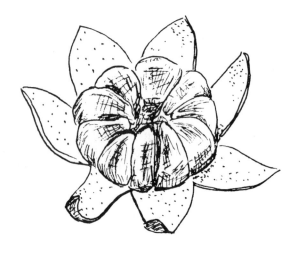

THE KUMQUAT . . . Taste buds educated by the tropics eat the raw kumquat whole — skin and all.

Thinly sliced, unpeeled kumquats can be added to Ambrosia or to the more plebian fruit cocktail to surprise the taste buds.

Makes tiny sandwiches of sliced kumquat and cream cheese.

Remove the kumquat core and stuff the delicate peel with date and nut.

The kumquat appears during the Holidays and is a familiar garnish for citrus fruit gift baskets. Use its gold and green delicacy to deck your own halls. Anytime you can get them, the kumquat adds an eye-pleasing touch as a table decoration that whispers something about you as a host/hostess. When you're really feeling "arty" . . . make a kumquat flower bouquet to garnish a meat platter or brighten a buffet:

Lengthwise, cut kumquat in fourths, toward, and almost to, the stem end. Leave fruit portion to make the center of the flower. Peel petals ¾ of the way back and then chill in ice water for an hour or so to "open."

SPICED KUMQUATS

2 pounds kumquats

Slit washed kumquats across sections to prevent them from bursting open and to allow spices to penetrate. Cover with water, bring to a boil and cook until tender. Drain.

3 cups sugar
1 cup vinegar

Combine and pour over cooked kumquats. Bring to boil and cook briskly until fruit is clearing and syrup thickens.

2 cinnamon sticks
1 T whole cloves
1 T whole allspice
1 piece ginger

Make spice bag. (See Note 2, page 3.) Add spice bag to hot fruit and stir. Allow to stnd overnight to "plump." In the morning, boil again until kumquats are transparent and shining and syrup is thick. Cover tightly. Let stand again overnight. Reheat, remove spice bag, pack in pint jars and process for canning as in Note 1, page 8.

THE LIME . . . the emerald of the tropics

The crusaders, plagued by scurvy long before the long voyages of trade inflicted the disease on sailors, brought the lime back to Europe. One of my own ancestors, Denis de Verteuil, took part in one of those remarkable religious adventures. Though he and his companions failed to liberate Jerusalem, I like to think he was one of the pilgrims who returned with a few lime seeds tucked in his armour.

Not the best source of Vitamin C, the lime, however, is a natural sea traveller as it keeps a long time and does not bruise easily. Though some Captains recognized as early as the sixteen hundreds that those of the crew who quenched their thirst with limes were healthier, it was not until 1795 that the juice became compulsory on all British ships. The practice that gave the Englanders the nickname "Limey" was still in force in 1955, the last year I myself served on one of the old Empire's ships.

Dr. Henry Perrine, physician-botanist, planted the first Florida lime trees on Indian Key where he had gone to conduct experiments in tropical fruit growing in 1835. The Doctor was killed by Indians five years later, but his family survived by hiding in a turtle crawl beneath the burning house.

THERE ARE A HUNDRED AND ONE USES FOR A LIME . . . Use the juice, grate the peel or plant the seed and grow a tree. Slice it, wedge it or quarter it. Here are just a few ideas:

Of course, use lime with tea, iced or hot.

Serve lime wedges with Florida oysters on the half shell. Squeeze juice on oyster before eating.

Lime juice preserves the color of avocados, mangos, bananas and apples; enhances the flavor of melons and papayas.

A generous dash of lime juice in a cup of beef consomme, adds excitement to an old stand-by.

The afficiando imbibes tequilla ritually with salt at the base of the thumb and a wedge of lime held gallantly between thumb and forefinger. One licks the salt, tosses off a shot of the cactus liquor and sucks the lime, all in one easy, fluid motion.

Rub fish with lime before cooking.

Put a slice of lime pierced with a whole clove in the bottom of your tea cup.

Put a dollop of slightly thawed limeade concentrate over your bowl of breakfast berries.

Float very thin slices of lime in clear soup.

Squeeze lime juice over melon balls and top with shredded coconut for a palate pleasing end to a luncheon.

Before broiling chicken, "wash" in water to which lime juice has been added.

USE LIME WITH FISH

LIME BUTTER SAUCE . . . a spread for poached fish.

¼ cup lime juice
1 T plus 1 t butter
½ t grated lime peel
dash tabasco

Blend.

PICANTO LIME FISH SAUCE

¾ cup lime juice
½ cup finely chopped green onion

Marinate onions in lime juice for 1 hour. Drain. Reserve juice.

2 T butter

Saute onions in butter. Do not allow to brown any shade.

1 pinch cayenne
2 cloves garlic, put through press
freshly ground black pepper
seasoned salt

Add seasonings, simmer at lowest heat possible for 10 minutes. Remove from heat, add lime juice and serve hot over fish.

FLORIDA LIME SEVICHE . . . Use any variety of white meat fish, cleaned and cut into bite size pieces. The less adventurous eaters reject the thought of eating "raw" fish, but in reality Seviche is not raw at all but is rather "cooked" by the lime acid.

DICED RAW FISH

2 cups lime juice
⅓ cup finely chopped onion
3 cloves garlic, finely chopped
2 hot peppers, finely chopped
1 t chili powder
1 t salt
1 t sugar
¼ t oregano
freshly ground black pepper
¼ cup olive oil

Combine all ingredients and mix well. Add fish pieces, cover tightly and allow to marinate in refrigerator overnight.

You can serve seviche as an appetizer or as an accompaniment to end-of-the-day cocktails. It's great for lunch or at poolside. In place of fish, you may substitute scallops.

Fifteenth century sea powers planted limes at strategic locations as growing medical stations.

FISH TROPIQUE

1 pound fish filets

2 cups water	Allow to marinate at room temperature for 1 hour.
½ cup lime juice	
1 t MSG salt	

2 T olive oil	Brown vegetables gently in oil.
2 onions, sliced	
1 tomato, sliced	
2 cloves garlic, chopped finely	

pinch cayenne	Add these ingredients and allow to simmer for 15 minutes. Add fish drained of marinade. Place lime slice over filets and cook for some 10 minutes, covered. Fish should be flaky. Strain stock and serve in side boat along with fish.
2 bay leaves	
2 T chopped parsley	
½ t thyme	
1 cup water	
1 cup chablis	

1 lime, sliced

LIME SALAD DRESSINGS

FRENCH LIME DRESSING

¼ cup lime juice	Blend.
1 t dry mustard	
1 t paprika	
1 t seasoned salt	
1 T grated onion	
1 t celery seed	
½ cup sugar	

1 cup salad oil	Add infinitely slowly to above mixture, with blender turned on.

HONEY LIME . . . for fruit salad

1 egg, slightly beaten	Put in saucepan.

½ cup lime juice	Add these ingredients and cook until slightly thick, stirring constantly. Remove from heat and cool.
½ cup honey	
½ t salt	
freshly ground white pepper	
1 t ginger, optional	
1 cup sour cream	Fold in and chill.

Make Fresh Florida Limeade with equal amounts of juice and superfine sugar: Garnish with a sprig of mint or a thin slice of lime astride the glass rim. For that special touch when you're entertaining your old neighbor from back home, dip the glass edge in egg white, then in sugar and put in freezer until ready to use.

LIME ACCOMPANIMENTS

LIME COCKTAIL SAUCE . . . a dip for shellfish.

1 cup ketchup
2 T lime juice
10 drops Tabasco
1 small grated onion
½ t salt
1 T horseradish
1 t chopped parsley

Mix all ingredients thoroughly.

LIME PEPPER SAUCE . . . to sprinkle in bean soup or on fish filets . . . to "pica" anything.

2 cups fresh lime juice, strained
1 T salt
2 hot peppers, whole

Combine ingredients in jar with tight cover. Shake well. Allow to stand at room temperature for 20 odd days.

LIME HOLLANDAISE

1 cup butter, melted and cooled

4 egg yolks, beaten until thick
½ t salt
pinch of cayenne

Combine these ingredients. Add small amount of butter, beating briskly by hand or at high speed electrically.

2 T lime juice

Add small amount of lime juice, again beating. Alternate butter and juice until munitions are exhausted.

This Hollandaise keeps well in the refrigerator, but do not re-heat.

LIME BARBEQUE MARINADE

¼ cup lime juice
½ cup vinegar
½ cup oil
1 clove garlic, put through press
1 t MSG salt
freshly ground black pepper
crushed bay leaf

LIME CHICKEN MARINADE

1 T lime juice
1 t seasoned salt
½ t thyme
freshly ground black pepper
pinch cayenne
1 clove garlic, put through press
1 T finely chopped chives
1 t finely chopped parsley
dash Tabasco

Allow chicken pieces to stand in marinade in bowl for at least 1 hour. Brown the chicken in fat and add in marinade as desired.

A LIME PIE . . . the tart and the sweet alternate on the tongue to delight and refresh.

KEY LIME PIE

1 can sweetened condensed milk 3 egg yolks ½ cup fresh key lime juice	Beat ingredients together until thick and smooth.
1 baked pie shell	Pour mixture in pie shell.
3 egg whites ¼ t cream of tartar ½ t vanilla 6 T superfine sugar	Make meringue and spread over pie filling. Bake to brown, then chill before serving.

A key lime pie that is green is not a key lime pie. The Florida Cracker purist insists on the yellow pie made from true key limes. The trick is to squeeze them while they're in season, freeze the juice in ice cube trays, store them in freezer bags, and you'll have Key Lime Pie all year round.

LIME CHEESECAKE

2 8-oz. packages cream cheese 2 8-oz. packages cream cottage cheese 1½ cups sugar 4 eggs	Blend, electrically if possible, until frothy.
3 T flour 3 T cornstarch grated peel of 1 lime	Mix well together.
1 pint sour cream ¼ cup melted butter 1½ T lime juice 1 t vanilla	Mix these ingredients with flour mixture and beat until smooth. Add cheese mixture and again beat until smooth.
1 graham cracker crust	Put filling in crust and bake at 325 for 1 hour, then turn oven off and leave cake in oven for another 2 hours. Chill.

TART LIME CHIFFON PIE

4 egg yolks, slightly beaten ½ cup superfine sugar 4 T lime juice	Beat these ingredients together in top of double boiler. Cook until thick.
½ T unflavored gelatin, softened in ⅓ cup cold water	Add to mixture and allow to cool.
4 egg whites ½ cup superfine sugar 1 baked pie shell	Beat whites until stiff and add sugar gradually. Fold into cooled mixture. Pour into pie shell and chill before serving.

LIME DRINKS . . . with rum

The planter's verandah companion, often the navy's courage. Captain Hook in Treasure Island confessed "Rum's been both mother and wife to me." The pirates sang "Yo ho ho and a bottle of rum," the ladies of the Temperance movement attacked Demon Rum.

Rum is the mainstay of one of the oldest trades in the world and our not so Pure ancestors exchanged New England salt fish for Caribbean rum.

Rum is a derivative of sugar cane. Make dark brown sugar, light brown sugar, then white sugar. Throw away the molasses extracted and finish up with rum. Natives that work in the last phase in the islands are hard put to remain sober.

Here are Florida versions of familiar and not so familiar rum concoctions:

PALM BEACH PLANTERS PUNCH

Shake together 1 T lime juice, 1 T grenadine, dash curacao, 1 generous jigger dark rum. Strain into tall glass with ice. Add soda to fill. Garnish with stick of fresh pineapple joined to cherry with toothpick.

FLORIDA YACHTSMAN'S DAIQUIRI

In shaker, place 1 cube sugar. Douse with 1 T lime juice and dissolve with spoon. Add a generous jigger of light rum and shake with ice cubes. Strain into on-the-rocks glass over ice and serve.

For frozen daiquiri, multiply above recipe times number to be served and put ingredients in blender. Add ½ cup cracked ice for each drink and mix at high speed until mixture "snows." Serve immediately in stem glass.

GOLD COAST FIVE O'CLOCKER

Put 2 T superfine sugar in cocktail glass and add teakettle boiling water to dissolve. Add generous jigger of dark rum and the juice of half a lime. Add crushed ice, top with strip of lime peel.

NAPLES ENTERTAINER . . . serves 8 . . . use tall glasses

Melt ¼ cup sugar in the juice of two limes. Add 1 cup rum, ¼ cup grenadine and 1 large bottle soda. Frost glasses by dipping edge into lime juice, then into saucer of superfine sugar. Fill with ice cubes and pour in mixture.

OTHER LIME DRINKS

RUM AND COKE

The old Cuba Libre, now called by another name among that country's Florida expatriates, is not the same without a neat wedge of lime. Rum and coca-cola and fresh lime, a good drink for people who don't drink much.

VODKA AND TONIC . . . below standard without fresh lime

No finer, lighter drink exists for the leisure of a tropic cocktail hour in summer. Pour vodka over ice, add tonic. Go round the glass rim with the fruit side of a wedge of lime, then drop in the wedge.

Eating limes will not get you into the limelight which has to do with the mineral rather than the fruit.

SANGRIA . . . There are a thousand ways to make and to serve this fruited wine concoction. The permutations of method and ingredient is mind-boggling, but here is my favorite:

. . . Marinate a fruit mixture with a syrup made of ⅔ cup dry vermouth, 5 T superfine sugar, ½ t cinnamon.

½ **gallon dry, full bodied, red wine**
1 **orange, sections of, halved**
4 **thin slices lime**
8 **slices mango (from the freezer**
    out of season)
1 **banana, sliced**
1 **cup grapes, halved to**
    absorb wine
¼ **cup cubed papaya**
¼ **cup chunk pineapple**
	Add these ingredients and allow to stand one hour before serving in large, glass pitcher. Pour the wine as toasts are called for, then eat the wine-soaked fruit for dessert.

CAFE DE VACA

4 **cups coffee**	Keep hot over low fire.
2 **sticks cinnamon** 4 **whole cloves** ¼ **cup orange peel strips** 2 T **lime peel strips** ¼ **cup sugar** ½ **cup rum**	Heat to very hot, remove from fire and ignite, immediately pouring hot coffee in side of pan. When flames die down, strain coffee into cups.

HERE ARE SOME MIXED FRUIT DELIGHTS . . . classic and camp

AMBROSIA

4 **oranges, sections of** 1 **grapefruit, sections of** 2 **bananas, sliced** 2 T **superfine sugar** 2 T **lime juice** ½ **t almond extract** ½ **cup guava jelly**	Combine all ingredients and chill before serving. (Except coconut)
Grated coconut	Sprinkle with grated coconut.

AMBROSIA, CAREER GIRL STYLE

1 **cup fruit salad** ½ **cup orange concentrate**	Combine.
½ **cup sour cream** ¼ **cup guava jelly cubes**	Mix and top fruit.

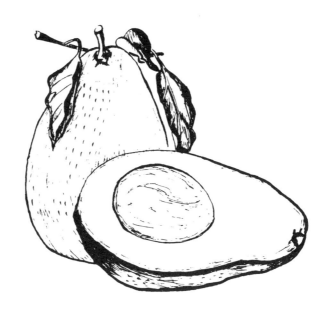

THE AVOCADO

Unlike most Florida fruits, the avocado is a native of the New World rather than the Old. The name is a corruption of the Aztec "ahuacatl" and the fruit was considered by those learned people as an aphrodisiac.

Florida avocados are the finest in the world and you can get them from August through October. Avocados never ripen on the tree but must be picked and allowed to soften for several days before eating. In the supermarket, avocados are mostly sold unripe, so you must plan several days in advance when the exotic "alligator pear" is part of your menu. The fruit will ripen some faster if wrapped in a brown paper bag.

Here are some avocado beauty tips:

1. Give yourself a fifteen minute facial with blended, ripe avocado.

2. Mix pureed avocado with non-detergent shampoo and warm water for a restorative hair treatment.

3. Put avocado crescents under the eyes for 15 minutes of relaxation to smooth out lines, shrink bags.

4. If you tend to be chubby and care, remember that the avocado has a high oil content than any fruit save the olive.

PREPARING THE AVOCADO

Halve unpeeled avocado lengthwise and pull apart by twisting halves in opposing directions. Coax out pit. If this proves difficult, strike sharply with knife blade and extract. Now peel the fruit halves. Like tomatoes, avocados taste better at room temperature and like apples, the color and texture of the avocado is preserved by lime juice.

An avocado is ripe when the fruit "gives" inside the peel when held in the palm of the hand.

Once the avocado is prepared thusly, you can stuff it, slice it (cross-wise), dice it, puree it — even bake it. Here's how:

SLICED AVOCADO

1. Add avocado slices to your favorite tossed salad.

2. Slice avocado and arrange on lettuce bed. Sprinkle generously with vinaigrette-type dressing.

3. Arrange shellfish salad on lettuce bed. Arrange sliced avocado over the salad, then garnish with herring filets, capers, olives, quartered hard-boiled eggs.

4. Marinate the following overnight in ½ cup red wine vinegar, ¾ cup sugar, salt and pepper to taste: 1 can kidney beans, 1 can green beans, 1 can yellow wax beans (all drained), 1 sweet onion cut in rings, 1 green pepper cut in rings. Add sliced avocado within an hour of serving.

5. Alternate slices of avocado and grapefruit sections on bed of lettuce. Dress with 1 part grapefruit juice blended with 2 parts salad oil to which has been added a pinch of sugar, some celery seed, freshly ground white pepper and salt to taste.

6. Make marinade by blending ¼ cup salad oil, ¼ cup chablis, 2 T wine vinegar, ½ t sugar, ¼ t seasoned salt, ¼ t basil. Pour over 1 avocado, sliced, 1 cup fresh sliced mushrooms and 1 thinly sliced red onion. Allow to marinate for 2-3 hours, drain and serve.

7. AVOCADO-SPINACH SALAD

Fresh Spinach, washed, drained, snipped to pieces with kitchen shears
½ cup water chestnuts, sliced
2 cups fresh bean sprouts
2 hard boiled eggs, diced
5 slices of bacon, fried crisp and crumbled
1 red onion, sliced thin and separated into rings
1 avocado, sliced and sprinkled with lime juice

Toss all ingredients with Papaya Seed Dressing, Page 61

STUFFED AVOCADO

Prepare as above. Serve at room temperature on bed of lettuce greens, in nest of cottage cheese or comfortably tucked in a suitable salad dish. Serve the baked stuffed avocado recipes on a bed of rice or noodles or on a serving platter.

1. Stuff avocado half with equal parts softened cream cheese and fresh dairy cream. Blend together with chopped green onions, chopped parsley and chopped pickles. Add salt and pepper to taste, blend until smooth and stuff avocado cavity. Top with flower made of thinly sliced olive and a center of pimiento.

2. Stuff with diced, cooked shrimp dressed with mayonnaise and capers.

3. CRABMEAT SALAD STUFFING Combine ½ pound crab meat with 1 cup finely chopped celery and just enough mayonnaise to bind. Spoon into avocado cavity and serve with the following dressing: Mix well 1 cup mayonnaise, ½ cup sour cream, ½ t Worcestershire sauce, dash Tabasco, ¼ t crushed rosemary, 2 T chili sauce.

4. TUNA FISH STUFFING Combine 1 can white tuna in water, drained and flaked apart, ½ cup sliced water chestnuts, ¼ cup mayonnaise, 1½ t soy sauce, ½ t curry powder, dash Tabasco, 3 T finely chopped onion, 2 T finely chopped pickle.

5. SHELLFISH STUFFING Use doggie bag shrimp, lobster or crabmeat or any combination thereof. Dice the seafood and mix with chopped hard-boiled eggs. Make the following dressing:

2 T hot chicken bouillon **1 t curry powder**	Allow powder to dissolve in liquid.
1 egg yolk **1 T lime juice** **½ t dry mustard** **freshly ground white pepper** **½ t seasoned salt**	Blend these ingredients.
1 cup oil **1 T boiling water**	Add oil, a drop at a time at first, then by the tablespoon as sauce thickens. Add diluted curry powder and the boiling water while blending.

Moisten diced seafood with dressing, stuff the avocado half, then top with additional dressing. Garnish with paprika.

6. Heat 3 T currant jelly, 3 T catsup, 3 T wine vinegar, 6 T consomme in saucepan. Pour in avocado cavity and serve like cantaloupe.

7. Halve avocado cross-wise and prepare as directed on page 42. Blend 1 3oz. package cream cheese, 1 T heavy dairy cream, 1 T grated onion, 1 T finely chopped parsley. Stuff avocado halves, chill and cut ⅓" thick rings. Use as garnish or on salad plate.

DICED AVOCADO

1. Substitute diced avocado for croutons on soup for a gourmet difference.

2. AVOCADO-PINEAPPLE

¼ **cup olive oil** 1 **t seasoned salt**	Mix well.
1 **large avocado, diced** 1 **fresh pineapple, diced** 1 **small sweet onion, cut into rings**	Mix these ingredients with salted olive oil and allow to stand for 5 minutes.
⅓ **cup wine vinegar**	Add vinegar, toss and chill for one hour before serving.

3. AVOCADO-TOMATO

2 **avocados, diced and sprinkled** **with lime juice** 2 **tomatoes, peeled and diced** 2 **pounds cooked shrimp, diced** **seasoned salt** **freshly ground black pepper**	Mix these ingredients.
1 **egg, well beaten** 2 **T wine vinegar** ½ **t dry mustard** ½ **t seasoned salt** 1 **T tomato paste** ½ **t chili powder** ½ **cup stuffed olives, chopped fine** 2 **grated onion** 1 **T basil**	Blend these ingredients, in electric blender if possible.
1 **cup oil**	Add oil while blender is turned on, a drop at a time until mixture begins to thicken, then a tablespoon at a time.
1 **T boiling hot water**	Add water to lighten.
	Toss avocado/shrimp mixture in dressing, chill and serve.

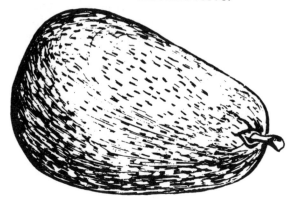

PUREED AVOCADO

GUACAMOLE Purists pronounce it "wah-kah-mo'-lay." Serve it as a dip for chips, fresh vegetables or cold shrimp and in place of sour cream with baked potato.

1 very ripe avocado, chopped
1 small tomato, peeled, seeded
   and chopped
2 T grated green onion
1 T lime juice
pinch of garlic powder
Tabasco to taste
Seasoned salt to taste
Freshly ground black pepper

Blend all ingredients, preferably in electric blender.

I make my guacamole as my avocados ripen (I have a wonderfully bountiful avocado tree), pour it from the blender into the on-the-rocks size plastic glasses, seal same in clear freezer bags, thaw as I need them and usually serve in as-is container for impromptu patio gatherings.

2. AVOCADO CELERY STUFFING

1 3 oz. package cream cheese
1 T thick dairy cream
1 cup avocado, chopped
1 T chopped chives

Blend all ingredients.

3. AVOCADO DIP

1 ripe avocado, chopped
2 T minced onion
1 clove garlic, put through press
pinch chili powder
freshly ground black pepper
½ t seasoned salt
2 T bacon bits
⅓ cup mayonnaise

Blend all ingredients.

4. AVOCADO SHRIMP COCKTAIL SAUCE

1 ripe avocado, chopped
¼ cup sour cream
1 T lime juice
½ t seasoned salt
1 T onion juice
1 T horseradish
dash horseradish

Blend all ingredients.

5. AVOCADO-HAM MUSHROOM STUFFING

1 ripe avocado, chopped
1 can deviled ham
¼ cup mayonnaise
2 T grated onion
freshly ground black pepper
seasoned salt to taste

Blend all ingredients.

6. AVOCADO-CLAM DIP

1 ripe avocado, chopped
1 T lime juice
1 T grated onion
½ t seasoned salt
freshly ground black pepper
dash Tabasco
¼ cup mayonnaise
1 can minced clams, drained

Blend all ingredients.

7. AVOCADO CORN ON THE COB BUTTER

½ ripe avocado, chopped
½ pound butter, softened
1 T chopped parsley
½ t oregano
½ t savory
1 T lime juice
dash chili powder

Blend all ingredients and spread on hot corn.

8. AVOCADO SALAD DRESSING

1 ripe avocado, chopped
3 T grated onion
2 T lime juice
1 T Worcestershire sauce
½ t seasoned salt
freshly ground black pepper
1 cup mayonnaise
pinch dry mustard

Blend all ingredients.

9. AVOCADO BLEU CHEESE SALAD DRESSING

1 ripe avocado, chopped
1 8 oz. package cream cheese
1 cup sour cream
2 T lime juice
1 T Pickapeppa sauce
2 oz. bleu cheese, crumbled

Blend first 5 ingredients, then add crumbled cheese by stirring only.

10. AVOCADO MEAT LOAF TOPPING

1 ripe avocado, chopped
¼ cup mayonnaise
⅓ cup chili sauce
dash cayenne
1 small onion, chopped fine
1 T lime juice

SCALLOPS ON THE AVOCADO HALF SHELL

1 pound scallops

Steam for 5 minutes or until tender.

2 avocados, halved, sprinkled
  with lime juice

3 T butter
1 small onion, finely chopped

Saute onion in butter, taking care onion does not brown.

1 cup white sauce

Add white sauce.

2 T chopped parsley
½ t seasoned salt
freshly ground white pepper
dash garlic powder
1 egg, slightly beaten

Combine these ingredients and add to white sauce mixture. Add scallops. Stir until mixture comes to boil and cook for 2 minutes over lowered heat. Spoon mixture into avocado cavities and bake at 350 until avocado is heated through. Serve on bed of rice.

POACHED FISH WITH AVOCADO SAUCE

2 pounds fish filets (white meat)
Lime juice

Wash fish filets in lime juice.

1 onion, sliced
2 carrots, sliced
2 celery stalks, cut in short strips
1 t seasoned salt
freshly ground black pepper

Layer these vegetables in heavy pan.

1 can chicken consomme'
1 clove garlic, put through press
1 bay leaf
1 t rosemary
1 t thyme

Blend these ingredients and add to vegetables. Bring to boil, then lower heat and simmer slowly for 20 minutes, covered. Add fish filets and cook until flakey.

2 avocados, chopped
2 T lime juice
1 T grated onion
1 t seasoned salt
freshly ground black pepper
3 T mayonnaise

Blend these ingredients and serve with fish like tartar sauce.

AN AVOCADO SANDWICH . . . The Earl of Sandwich was having such a run of luck at the gambling table that he called for his manservant to bring him a piece of meat between bread. From such a beginning came today's luscious sandwiches. Here are some ideas for the most exotic of all sandwiches:

1. Slices of avocado on your tuna sandwich will bring this homemaker's regular to life.

2. Pureed and seasoned avocado used as a spread enhances a sandwich made of leftover chicken or fish.

3. How about a grilled avocado and cheese?

4. Or a bacon, lettuce, tomato AND avocado?

5. Egg and Avocado. Remove yolk from half a dozen hard boiled eggs and blend the yellows with 1 small finely chopped onion, 2 T lime juice, 1 t seasoned salt, pinch cayenne, 2 T finely chopped chives, freshly ground black pepper. Dice whites of eggs and a large avocado. Mix with yolk mixture, adding mayonnaise to achieve consistency desired.

6. BROILED AVOCADO AND TUNA

**4 hamburger buns, split
  and buttered**

1 cup mashed avocado **¼ cup finely diced green peppers** **2 T grated onion** **½ cup mayonnaise**	Blend these ingredients.
1 can white tuna in water, drained and mashed with fork	Add tuna to blended mixture and blend once more. Spread mixture on buns and broil until hot and lightly brown. Heat tops and cover sandwich.

7. AVOCADO SANDWICH SUPREME

¼ cup buttermilk **½ cup mayonnaise** **2 T grated onion** **1 t Pickapeppa Sauce** **1 clove garlic, put through press** **dash seasoned salt** **1 cup bleu cheese**	Blend these ingredients.
1 cup bleu cheese, crumbled	Stir in this cheese without blending.
4 slices toast	Spread mixture on toast.
4 slices bacon, fried **lettuce** **1 avocado, sliced**	Place 2 pieces bacon on each sandwich half. Top with lettuce, then add avocado layer. Reserve extra dressing for repeating recipe soon.

CRABMEAT STUFFED BAKED AVOCADO

2 avocados, halved and sprinkled
  with lime juice

1 stick of butter   Saute onion in butter but do not allow to
1 small onion, finely chopped   brown at all.

2 T flour   Make roux with flour and cook for 2 minutes.

3 cups milk, scalded   Add milk, a small amount at a time, guarding
                          against lumping. Cook and stir until smooth
                          and thick. Remove from heat.

1 pound lump crabmeat   Combine these ingredients and add sauce. Fill
1 t prepared mustard   avocado cavities with mixture, sprinkle with
1 T Pickapeppa Sauce   Parmesan cheese and bake at 400 for 15 min-
                          utes or until avocado is heated through.

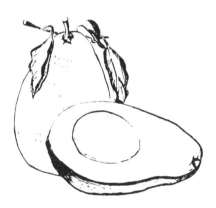

CURRY SHRIMP STUFFED AVOCADO IN AVOCADO RICE BED

1 cup diced green mango   Saute mango in butter without browning.
½ stick butter

2 clove garlic, put through press   Add these ingredients and saute without
1 small onion, grated   browning.
2 t curry powder

1 cup chicken broth   Add these ingredients to sauteed mixture.
2 T lime juice   Cook carefully until mixture begins to thicken.
½ t seasoned salt
freshly ground black pepper

2 pounds uncooked shrimp,   Add shrimp and cook until seafood is tender.
  beheaded, etc.

2 avocados, halved and sprinkled   Stuff avocado cavities and bake until heated
  with lime juice   through.

Hot, cooked rice for 4   When rice is done, add diced avocado and
1 avocado, diced   replace lid immediately to allow avocado rice
                          to steam. When done, make bed of rice on
                          serving platter, add stuffed avocado halves
                          and serve.

BAKED AVOCADO CUBANO

2 diced avocados
1 cup stale breadcrumbs
½ cup grated swiss cheese
1 T onion juice
½ t seasoned salt
freshly ground black pepper
pinch of sugar
1 t chopped parsley
1 cup white sauce
2 eggs, beaten

Combine all ingredients in buttered casserole. Bake at 325 for some 15 to 20 minutes or until heated through.

AVOCADO OMELET

2 T butter
¼ cup taco chips

Soften chips in butter in skillet. Use low heat.

6 eggs, well beaten
½ t seasoned salt

Add eggs and allow to set.

1 cup grated cheese

Remove eggs from heat and cover with cheese. Place pan in 300 oven until cheese melts.

1 cup avocado, diced
¼ cup dairy cream
1½ t lime juice
2 T green pepper, finely chopped
1 T onion, finely chopped
pinch of salt
pinch of chili powder

Combine these ingredients and layer over melted cheese. Return to oven for some 6 minutes, fold in two when done and serve.

AVOCADO SOUP

2 cups chicken consomme'
1 avocado, chopped then mashed

Mix well and heat slowly to simmer.

2 eggs, beaten
1 cup white sauce

Blend these ingredients and beat well. Add 4 T consomme' to egg mixture, 1 T at a time to initiate heating, then combine 2 mixtures and serve.

AVOCADO VI

2 avocados, chopped
½ cup sour cream
1¼ cup condensed beef soup
   undiluted
1 t seasoned salt
1 T lime juice
4 green onions with tops,
   chopped fine
2 tomatoes, peeled, seeded
   and diced
dash cayenne

Blend all ingredients. Chill before serving with garnish of parsley.

AVOCADO CAKE

1⅓ cups sugar   Cream together.
½ cup butter

2 eggs, well beaten   Add eggs and cream.

1 cup pureed avocado   Add avocado and cream until light and fluffy.

½ t cinnamon   Add these ingredients and beat.
½ t nutmeg, freshly ground
½ t allspice
½ t salt
1½ t baking soda

⅓ cup buttermilk   Add these ingredients and mix well.
½ cup chopped dates
¼ cup golden raisins
½ cup chopped walnuts

1½ cups all purpose flour, sifted   Add flour and mix thoroughly to a stiff batter. Turn into 9x9 greased baking dish and bake for 1 hour at 325 or until toothpick comes out clean.

1 pint heavy cream   Combine all ingredients in mixer and beat until stiff. Chill and serve dollop of this cream on each piece of avocado cake.
¼ cup light rum
pinch of salt
1 cup confectioners sugar

AVOCADO CREME

2 ripe avocados, chopped   Puree in blender.
2 T lime juice

3 T superfine sugar   Add sugar and blend until smooth.

2 jiggers light rum   Add rum and blend but only just long enough to make smooth. Over-blending can ruin. Pour into 4 wine glasses and chill before serving.

AVOCADO ICE CREAM

4 avocados, chopped   Puree in blender
2 T lime juice

6 egg yolks, well beaten   Cook in double boiler until mixture thickens.
1½ cups sugar
1 quart light cream
½ t salt
½ t almond extract
2 t vanilla

1 pint heavy cream   Blend with avocado. When egg yolk mixture cools, combine all ingredients and freeze.

THE MANGO . . . musty and exotic.

The mango was born at the foot of the Himalayas and may well be mankind's most anciently cultivated fruit. Trees have been known to live a hundred years and the fruit can be eaten green as chutney and in pies. Ripe, treat the fruit like a fresh peach.

The first mango tree to bear fruit in Florida was planted upon the Miami River during the Civil War and now there are over 50 varieties of the venerated fruit in this state. Florida's mango trees bear from May to September, but most fruit ripens in June and July.

The allergy sensitive should approach the mango with some caution. The juice is the culprit, but it is ubiquitous and on the face and hands or in the eye, it can cause skin eruptions and swelling.

SHOPPING TIPS Buy mangos that are firm and allow them to stand at room temperature until the fruit "gives." It is normal for some mango varieties to "speckle" when ripe and you should not be turned off by this. Though green mangos have their uses, it you intend to serve ripe, be certain ripening is complete, as underripening makes for an entirely different, and not desirable, taste.

In 1821, James Forbes who had been born in British Florida, grew up in Spanish Florida and would work for President James Monroe in taking possession of American Florida, wrote that the mango was "greatly esteemed . . . on account of its invigorating odour and resinous substance, which are said to be beneficial in pulmonary complaints.

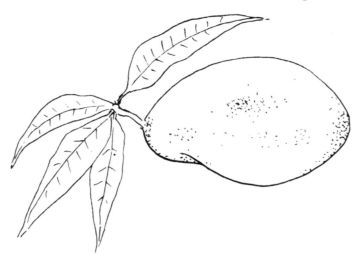

PREPARING THE MANGO

Chill before peeling and peel from the small end. The mango pit is not freestone, but rather clings to the meat around it. Therefore, cut as large a slice as possible from the top of the fruit, avoiding the pit; turn over in the palm and slice off the second half. Cut meat from ends. Like licking the bowl, the preparer is now priviledged to lean over the sink with the pit in hand to remove the last of the fruit meat from the pit, slurping and dripping in infinite enjoyment.

TO FREEZE . . . ripe mangos

Pre-freeze slices on cookie sheet or equivalent, placing so fruit slices do not touch each other. When fruit is frozen, remove, place in freezer container and store. Bite-size slices are good to eat frozen or partially frozen and this method allows you to remove amount desired from your supply.

. . . green mangos

Boil whole green mangos until skin splits open. Peel while hot and scrape pulp from pit. Blend mango flesh with an equal amount of sugar and package immediately for freezing since green mangos contain high levels of pectin and it is not advisable to allow it to set. This frozen mixture can be used for sauces and pie fillings.

EAT FRESH SLICED MANGOS . . . plain like a bowl of peaches or with a few drops of lime juice.

OR

For each mango sliced, sprinkle with ¼ cup confectioners sugar and ⅓ cup rum. Chill and use as topping for ice cream. A gourmet sensation denied to most is this rare dish. Fold sour cream into vanilla pudding and spoon a dollop of this on a bowl of fresh, sliced mangos.
Add honey and lime juice to a bowl of fresh sliced mangos and allow to marinate overnight.

GREEN MANGO PIE

4 cups sliced green mangos

Parboil mangos until slices are limber.

1 pastry shell, with top crust

Arrange mango slices in pastry shell.

1¼ cups sugar
½ t nutmeg
½ t cinnamon
1 stick butter

Mix sugar and spices and sprinkle over mangos. Dot with butter and cover with top crust, making openings with knife. Bake 45 to 50 minutes in a 350 oven.

RIPE MANGO COBBLER

1½ quarts thickly sliced
     ripe mangos
3 cups sugar

Allow sugar to draw syrup. After marinating sufficiently, heat.

2 T cornstarch
1½ cups cold water
1 t freshly ground mutmeg

Dissolve cornstarch in 2 T of the cold water, then add remaining water. Add mixture to heated fruit. Add nutmeg. Bring to boil then allow to bubble, stirring constantly for 1 minute. Pour mixture into greased, deep-dish glass baking container.

½ stick butter

Dot with butter.

2⅓ cup biscuit mix
3 T sugar
⅓ cup cream

Mix all ingredients with fork to a soft dough. Knead 8 times on lightly floured cloth-covered board. Drop dough by the spoonful onto hot fruit. Bake 20 minutes at 400 and serve warm with cream.

MANGO PIE IN BOURBON PASTRY SHELL

1 cup flour, unsifted measurement
¼ t salt

Sift together.

⅓ cup oil

Add to blend to consistency of corn meal.

4 T bourbon, ice cold

Add bourbon to make a stiff dough. Place on floured surface and roll ⅛" thick. Arrange in pie tin and finish edge.

2 cups diced mango
1½ cups sugar
3 T flour
3 egg yolks
1 t vanilla

Combine these ingredients and turn into pie shell. Bake at 350 for 1 hour. Remove from heat.

3 egg whites
¼ t cream of tartar
½ t vanilla
6 T superfine sugar

Beat egg whites until stiff but not dry. Add other ingredients to make meringue. Spread over pie filling to seal and return to oven to brown topping.

RECK'S MANGO COMPOTE

3 ripe mangos, sliced 2 grapefruit, sections of and juice can apricot nectar 3 T lime juice ½ cup sugar	Allow these ingredients to marinate overnight.
3 bananas, sliced	Add bananas and allow the family free rein to have a refreshing bowl for breakfast, all-day snack time, lunch, dinner dessert.

MANGO ICE CREAM

3 cups pureed mango fruit ¾ cup sugar pinch of salt 2 T lime juice ½ t almond extract	Combine and stir until sugar is dissolved. Freeze for 45 minutes.
2 egg whites, well beaten 2 T sugar	Add sugar gradually and beat until stiff.
2 egg yolks, well beaten	Add egg yolks.
½ pint whipping cream, whipped	Fold into egg mixture, then add mango mixture and freeze.

MANGO ICE CREAM TOPPING

½ stick butter	Melt in chafing dish until bubbling.
scant ¼ cup sugar	Add sugar, stirring until blended.
1 strip orange peel 1 strip lemon peel	Add peels and allow to heat 1 minute.
¾ cup orange juice	Add juice and heat.
2 cups diced ripe mango	Add fruit and stir until heated through.
1 scant jigger Kirsch 1 large jigger Grand Marnier	Stir in.
1 jigger brandy, heated	Pour over fruit and ignite. Spoon over vanilla ice cream in individual dishes and serve.

MANGO CAKE . . . here are filling and frosting recipes for your favorite

¾ cup mango puree ¾ cup sugar 3 T cornstarch dash salt 1 egg yolk 3 T lime juice 1 t grated orange peel	Blend these ingredients and cook in double boiler until thick, stirring constantly. Remove from heat.
1 T butter	Add butter and allow to cook before spreading between cake layers.
1 cup sugar ⅓ cup water ¼ t cream of tartar dash salt	Bring these ingredients to boil, stirring until sugar dissolves.
2 egg whites, unbeaten	In electric mixer, pour sugar syrup over egg whites slowly, with patience, beating constantly until stiff peaks form. (About 7 minutes.)
⅔ cup finely diced mango fruit	Add mango fruit and beat until you achieve desirable spreading consistency. Spread frosting over all three cake layers that have been spread with filling.

MANGO ANGEL FOOD CAKE TOPPING

3 cups pureed mango fruit 2 T orange concentrate ½ t vanilla Pinch of salt ½ cup confectioners sugar	Blend all ingredients.
1 cup whipping cream, whipped	Fold in whipped cream and chill before serving.

MANGO TAPIOCA . . . the permeating flavor of the mango enhances tapioca

1½ cups pureed mango ½ cup sugar	Allow sugar to draw mango juice for 1 hour. Drain, preserving juice.
water	Add enough water to mango juice to make 2 cups liquid.
¼ cup quick-cooking tapioca ¼ t salt	In saucepan, bring mango liquid and these ingredients to boil, then remove from heat. Add fruit pulp.
2 T lime juice	Add lime juice and mix well. Allow pudding to cool, stirring from time to time to prevent skim from forming.

GREEN MANGO CHUTNEY

1 pound diced green mango fruit **salt**	Salt mango, cover with cloth and allow to dry in sunny window for 1 day.
2 T dry chilis **2 T mustard seed** **1 T ginger root** **6 cloves garlic, halved**	Place spices in sachet (See note 2, page 8)
2 cups vinegar	Soak sachet in vinegar for 15 minutes.
1 t seasoned salt **1 pound dark brown sugar**	Heat vinegar over low heat, add salt and then sugar and stir until sugar is dissolved. Bring to boil carefully and simmer for 15 minutes. Cool to room temperature.
¾ cup raisins	Add raisins.

RIPE MANGO CHUTNEY

5 cups finely chopped mango fruit	
2 cups vinegar	Place in large, heavy pan.
6 whole cloves **2 cinnamon pieces**	Place spices in sachet (See Note 2, page 8) Soak sachet in vinegar for 15 minutes. Heat slowly.
4 cups dark brown sugar	Add sugar, stirring until syrup forms. Add mango pulp, bring to boil and cook, stirring constantly, for 10 minutes. Lower heat.
dash salt **¼ t chili powder**	Add these seasonings and simmer for 2 hours, stirring occasionally.
¼ cup raisins	Cool to room temperature and then add raisins.

CANNING

If you wish to "put up" your chutney, see Note 1, page 8. Do allow your chutney to stand overnight before packing in sterilized jars and do leave ½" head room at the top of the jar.

BREADFRUIT

There is absolutely no mystery to the time and the method of the breadfruit's arrival in the new world. As most people know, Captain William Bligh's first attempt to bring the breadfruit to the new world ended in mutiny, hangings, murders and the loss of his ship "Bounty".

Few are aware that Bligh, even before the court-martial was over, had obtained another ship and embarked on another voyage.

Every breadfruit in Florida is a descendant of one of the trees brought to the Americas on Bligh's second and successful expedition aboard the good ship "Providence".

You can substitute breadfruit in any recipe that calls for yams.

Bounty Souffle'

1 breadfruit, boiled and pureed
3 egg yolks

Mix together.

½ cup butter
1 cup milk
2 T grated cheese

Add these ingredients.

3 egg whiles, well beaten

Fold in egg whites, bake in well greased baking dish at 350 until crusty on the outside. (Inside will be soft.)

PAPAYA . . . familiarly known as the "pawpaw."

The papaya contains the magical PAPAIN, a digestive aid. Dried, the enzyme is the key ingredient in the commercial meat tenderizers you purchase at the supermarket. Since papaya trees bear year round in Florida's tropical south, why not use the real thing? I spent some years operating a charter boat in the Caribbean and I have seen one of the best cooks in the Islands under a leaf of banana leaves held up by 4 crooked posts, rubbing meat with slices of the green papaya. She also told me that meat wrapped in a bruised papaya leaf is succulently tender.

Never throw away the papaya seed, but rather refrigerate them in tightly closed jar. Ground, they are added to marinades and salad dressings for savour pleasure. Or bruise and soak in vinegar before adding.

Papaya juice is an antidote for digestive problems, but the fresh fruit should be approached by allergy prone fanciers with caution.

Native to Central America, the fruit's landing in Florida is not recorded, but probably came via early Incan trade. It is possible to plant a papaya seed, grow the plant, set it out, watch it mature and fruit, harvest the fruit, extract a seed and plant a new crop all in the same Florida year. Why not add a "pawpaw" tree to your backyard garden?

It is sometimes difficult for the uninitiated shopper to even recognize the papaya. It is anything but consistent, growing to sizes ranging from a walnut to 25 pounds and coming in all shapes — spherical, egg, pear, cylindrical.

THE PAPAYA . . .

. . . halved, seeded and sprinkled generously with lime juice . . . a great breakfast treat, appetizer or dessert.

. . . Biwi (British West Indian) connoisseurs eat the seeds along with the fruit.

. . . halvd, seed, sprinkle with lime juice and chill. When ready to serve, fill with fresh strawberries and top with a dollop of sour cream sprinkled with brown sugar.

. . . Peel. Cut in crosswise slices ½" thick and seed each slice. Fry in butter about 1 minute on each side and sprinkle each side with lime juice. Serve with bacon for a planter's breakfast.

. . . In your favorite mixed green salad, toss sliced papaya with papaya seed dressing (Recipe page 61)

. . . Add papaya slices to Ambrosia.

. . . Combine papaya balls, pineapple chunks, figs, pear nectar, 1 jigger Triple Sec, sliced banana. Chill and serve with sour cream sprinkled with brown sugar.

. . . Add diced papaya fruit to orange gelatin made with pineapple juice.

. . . Use 3 cups diced fresh papaya, 1 cup finely chopped celery, ¼ cup raisins and ½ cup chopped walnuts. Toss with mixture of ¼ cup mayonnaise, ¼ cup sour cream and ¼ cup crushed bleu cheese for a delightful fruit luncheon.

MIXED FRUIT SALADS

. . . On bed of lettuce, arrange grapefruit and orange sections around mound of cottage cheese. Garnish with pimiento.

. . . Fill a jar with assorted fruits cut into bite size pieces. Add rum to cover and allow to stand for several days. As you use, replace fruit and rum to keep the mixture thick and rich.

. . . Orange sections, cubed pineapple, mango pieces, honey and lime juice.

. . . Fill a half of papaya with orange sections, carambola slices, pistachio nuts; splash with papaya juice shot with Grand Marnier.

The famous papaya enzyme can make your complexion glow! Here's how: Remove fruit meat from halved, unpeeled papaya. Turn skins inside out and rub the meat side over your face and neck. Lie with skins on your cheeks for some 15 minutes or until you feel a drawing sensation. Rinse with warm, then cold, water. That's being good to yourself!

PAPAYA SEED SALAD DRESSING . . . intriguing — you'll learn to always keep a jar of it in the fridge!

1 cup red wine vinegar ½ cup superfine sugar 1 t dry mustard 1 T Pickapeppa sauce 1 t seasoned salt 2 T grated onion	Combine in electric blender.
2 cups salad oil	Add with blender on high, in infinitely fine stream. It is the little bit at a time that thickens dressing.
3 T papaya seeds	Add and blend for a short time, or only until dressing looks as if it contained coarsely ground pepper.

PAPAYA SEED MARINATE FOR FLANK STEAK . . . so good you will soon buy this cut (or London Broil) out of choice rather than economy.

½ cup salad oil 2 T red wine vinegar 2 T lime juice 1 package onion sour mix ½ t garlic powder ½ t rosemary ½ t basil 1 T Pickapeppa sauce 1 t salt freshly ground black pepper generous seeds from 1 fresh papaya	Combine all ingredients in blender, adding seeds last. Score steak or prick with fork and allow to marinate for 2 hours, turning frequently. Broil (on grill if possible) rare (I hope).

PICKLED PAPAYA . . . one of those condiments that makes a meal memorable . . . unique . . few people have had the pleasure of this taste.

4 cups sliced papaya fruit 3 cups sugar	Allow to marinate overnight. If fruit does not form enough juice to cover, add sufficient water to do so. In large and heavy pan, bring fruit to boil and allow to cook until syrup thickens. Drain, preserving liquid.
2 cinnamon sticks 1 T whole cloves 1 T whole allspice 1 cup vinegar	Make sachet of spices and boil in vinegar for 10 minutes. Add papaya fruit and boil for another 10 minutes. Let stand overnight. In the A.M., bring fruit mixture to boil in one pan, the syrup you preserved in another. Place fruit in hot, sterilized jars; add hot syrup. Process to can per (Note 1, page 8).

BAKED PAPAYA WITH CLAM STUFFING . . . the green papaya is treated like a vegetable.

2 green papayas, halved	Remove seeds and discard. Blanch fruit.
2 T butter 1 onion, diced ½ cup celery, diced 2 cloves garlic, finely diced	Saute vegetables in butter without browning.
1½ t poultry seasoning 1 t savory 1½ cups chicken broth	Add these ingredients. When liquid boils, remove from heat.
3 cups stale bread crumbs 1 can minced clams	Mix these two and add to liquid, tossing with fork until damp. Spoon mixture into papaya halves and bake for 1 hour, pouring an inch of boiling water around papayas. (Oven 325).
½ cup grated sharp cheese	When pulp is tender, sprinkle with cheese and bake an additional 25 minutes.

PAPAYA SAUCE FOR BAKED FISH

1 cup papaya juice ½ cup cream 3 T lime juice 1 t seasoned salt freshly ground white pepper pinch cayenne 1 T cornstarch 2 T papaya seeds	Combine all ingredients in blender. Cook until thick. Pour over fish in greased baking dish. Allow to marinate for 1 hour. Bake at 400 for 20 minutes or until fish flakes.

BAKED RIPE PAPAYA WITH CREAMED HAM

2 ripe papayas, halved and seeded	
2 T butter 2 T grated onion 3 T finely diced green pepper	Saute vegetables in butter but do not brown.
¼ cup biscuit mix	Add and mix well. Cook over low heat until mixture bubbles, stirring constantly.
1½ cups cream 1 can mushroom sour, undiluted	Add, heat to boiling and allow to cook for 1 minute.
1 T lime juice 2 cups diced ham 1 cup fresh sliced mushrooms	Remove from heat and add these ingredients. Fill papaya halves and bake at 350 for 50 minutes or until heated through. Serve on bed of rice.

PAPAYA FROZEN CREAM

1 3oz. package cream cheese, softened 1 T lime juice 4 T honey ¼ cup mayonnaise pinch of salt	Blend these ingredients.
1½ cups ripe diced papaya 1 avocado, diced and doused with lime juice ¼ cup chopped tart cherries	Add fruit and mix well.
½ pint whipping cream whipped	Fold in and freeze overnight for serving following day.

PAPAYA UPSIDE DOWN CAKE

1½ cups ripe, sliced papaya	Marinate overnight to draw syrup. Drain.
2 T butter ¼ cup dark brown sugar ⅓ cup pecans, whole pieces	Melt butter in square baking pan. Remove from heat and spread sugar into butter on bottom of pan. Arrange fruit and nuts in layer over this mixture.
1½ cups biscuit mix ½ cup sugar 1 egg ½ cup milk 2 T cooking oil 1 t vanilla	Blend all ingredients in electric mixer for 4 minutes at medium speed, using spatula constantly to scrape sides of bowl. Pour batter over sugar/fruit in baking pan and bake at 350 for some 35 minutes or until toothpick comes out clean. Invert on platter, allow pan to remain on cake for 2 minutes, then remove.

PAPAYA PIE

2 cups sliced papaya	Parboil fruit. Drain.
1 cup brown sugar 2 eggs, slightly beaten ½ t salt ½ t freshly ground ginger 1 t cinnamon ½ t allspice	Combine these ingredients and mix well.
2 cups light cream	Add milk, a little at a time, stirring to insure smoothness.
1 pastry shell, unbaked	Transfer to pastry shell and bake at 350 for 45 minutes or until fruit is tender.
1 package cream cheese 8 oz., softened 1 pint sour cream 1 t vanilla	Combine these ingredients. Chill and serve as topping for pie.

MIAMI MESMERIZER . . . a drink to liven up dull parties

1 t superfine sugar
2 T lime juice
1 jigger dark rum
1 jigger light rum
1 jigger pineapple juice
1 jigger papaya juice
dash apricot brandy

1 orange section
1 surinam cherry

Shake together all ingredients with ice and pour, unstrained, into tall, chilled glass. Garnish with orange section/cherry attached by a toothpick.

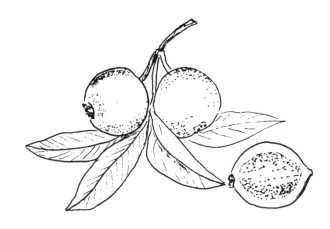

THE GUAVA . . . one of the richest sources known for Vitamin C.

. . . guava products were included in World War II emergency rations to build up resistance to infection.

. . . the guava was first grown commercially in Florida in 1912.

. . . the guava was discovered in 1526 by Spanish explorers of Central America.

FRESH GUAVA

. . . add slices to your favorite fresh fruit salad.

. . . make guava shortcake as you would strawberry shortcake for an exotic version of an old favorite.

. . . serve with cottage cheese as you would pineapple.

GUAVA BROWN BETTYE

2 cups bread crumbs ½ stick butter, melted	Toss to moisten crumbs and set aside.
1 cup sugar ¼ t cinnamon ¼ t nutmeg	Combine.
2 cups fresh guava, peeled, seeded and diced	Alternate layers of bread, sugar and fruit, in that order, until all munitions are exhausted.
¼ cup water 3 T lime juice	Combine and pour over layers.
½ stick butter	Dot with butter. Bake for 30 minutes at 350, covered with foil. Remove foil and bake for an additional 15 minutes or until brown. Serve with whipped cream.

GUAVA JELLY . . . the most famous guava product. Here's the way the state's Department of Agriculture recommends you make it:

2 **quarts firm, ripe guavas**
2 **quarts slightly green guavas**
2 **quarts water**

Wash guavas. Do not peel but remove blemishes and cut off ends. Bring to boil in water and cook 20 minutes. Strain through jelly bag, then re-heat liquid to boiling.

4 **cups sugar**

Add sugar and cook rapidly to 222 F by a candy thermometer (stirring constantly) with wooden paddle or spoon). Without a thermometer, use the "sheet" test to determine if jelly is done. Pour into clean jars and can according to directions on Note 1, page 8. (The "sheet" test is explained on page 11).

NOTE: Slow cooking makes jelly less attractively dark

USING GUAVA JELLY IN RECIPES

. . . Of course . . . with your favorite toast for breakfast . . . a classic . . . Guava jelly is delicious with cream cheese.

. . . Blend 3 T guava jelly, 1 T grated orange rind and 2 T prepared mustard to make a quick meat sauce for lamb.

GUAVA TEACAKE

vanilla wafers

Line 2-quart molding with half of vanilla wafers.

1 **jar guava jelly**

Spread a layer of guava jelly in mold over cookies, than add last half of wafers in another layer.

1 **jar citrus marmalade**

Spread over second cookie layer. Press firmly.

1 **cup strong tea**
¾ **cup light rum**

Bring to boil and pour over mixture. Allow to stand overnight and unmold. Cover with whipped cream and chill.

GUAVA SHELLS . . . are prepared guava halves and are the basis of many guava recipes. Here's how to make them, though, if you prefer, you may buy them canned in stores that cater to the Latin taste since they are a favorite dessert of Florida's Spanish population.

TO CAN GUAVA SHELLS

1. Choose firm, ripe guavas. Peel thinly or, if you want all the vitamins, leave unpeeled, merely removing blemishes. Cut in half.

2. With a spoon, scoop out seeds and soft pulp.

3. For each quart of shells, make 2 cups of syrup of 2 parts sugar and 1 part water.

4. Bring syrup to boil and add guava shells. Lower heat and cook some 3 to 5 minutes, depending on size of fruit.

5. Pack hot guava shells, cavity surface down, in overlapping layers in clean, hot jars, covering each layer with small amount of syrup.

6. Seal and process in hot water bath as directed in Note 1, page 8, for 15 minutes for pints, 20 minutes for quarts.

TO FREEZE GUAVA SHELLS

1. As in 1. above

2. As in 2. above

3. As in 3. above, but do not cook. If guavas are sweet, add lime juice. Blend well.

4. Pack guava shells in favorite freezer container and cover with syrup before freezing.

USING GUAVA SHELLS

. . . the traditional patrician way is to put a guava shell on a plate with a generous pat of cream cheese, add a few saltines, and serve.

. . . you can fill the shells with cottage cheese.

. . . you can top shells with sour cream and dust with fresh ground nutmeg.

. . . you can overflow with ice cream and garnish with nuts in syrup.

. . . blend softened cream cheese, a bit of milk to smooth, a pinch of salt, a spoon of orange concentrate, a squirt of lime juice, a pinch of grated orange peel and some chopped pecans. Fill shells with mixture.

GUAVA PASTE This is another way of preserving the guava. Making guava paste is a real art. My Mother, for instance, not only believed in a 24-hour set, but also in a 2-day sunning. I recommend that you do as I do — buy the commercial paste.

... alternate slices of guava paste and Monterey Jack cheese for a serendipitous snack.

GUAVA BREAD PUDDING

6 **cups stale bread cubes soaked in milk, drained**
2 **eggs, beaten**

Combine and spread in oblong baking pan.

1 **stick butter**

Dot with butter.

¼ **cup raisins**
½ **cup cream**
2 **cups sugar**
1 **cup small slices guava paste**
1 **T vanilla**

Combine these ingredients and distribute over bread mixture. Bake at 350 until brown and cooked around edges, but soft in the middle.

CARAMBOLA . . . called the star fruit as this is the shape they make when sliced.

. . . THEY ARE BEST EATEN RAW AND THEY MAKE AN EYE-OPENINGLY ATTRACTIVE ADDITION TO FRUIT SALADS AND COMPOTES.

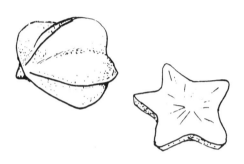

FRESH CARAMBOLA RELISH

2 cups sliced ripe carambola, seeded
¾ cup orange marmalade
½ cup chopped figs
pinch ginger
2 T lime juice
¼ cup superfine sugar

Combine all ingredients in blender until chopped. Refrigerate overnight before serving.

THE PLANTAIN . . . in some tradewind cultures, the plantain replaces both bread and potatoes.

PLANTAIN CHIPS

Peel, slice as thin as possible, fry in hot oil. Remove to paper towel and salt liberally while hot. Serve with avocado dip.

BOILED GREEN PLANTAIN

Peel, scrape, rub with lime juice to prevent discoloration, cook in boiling salted water about 30 minutes. Add butter, salt and pepper to taste.

SAUTEED RIPE PLANTAIN

Peel and quarter each plantain diagonally. Dip successively into beaten egg and bread crumbs. Brown in butter. Serve with brown sugar as dessert.

PLANTAIN IN SALAD

Steam plantains and allow them to cool. If using green plantain, slice, mix with vinaigrette. If using ripe plantain, slice, arrange on lettuce leaves, cover with mayonnaise and sprinkle with chopped nuts.

PLANTAIN STUFFING FOR BAKED FISH

2 ripe plantains
seasoned salt
2 sticks butter

Slice, saute and salt lightly, preserving butter in skillet.

1 can tomato sauce

Spread tomato mixture over the two halves of the open fish. Spread plantain over one half.

2 T grated coconut
4 T finely chopped mushrooms

Sprinkle plantain with coconut and mushrooms. Douse with butter left after cooking plantain. Close fish, bake in 400 oven for 10 minutes per pound (less if fish is under 3 lbs).

½ cup rum

Just before serving, boil rum to reduce by half, then pour it over fish to ignite.

FRESH FLORIDA FIGS . . . in cream for breakfast, a texture exciting addition to fruit salads.

FRESH FIG SUNDAE

8 figs, peeled and halved
2 jiggers rum
¼ cup honey
2 T lime juice
2 T caraway seed

Mix all ingredients, chill and serve over ice cream.

THE CALAMONDIN

CALAMONDIN HAM SAUCE . . . pour over thick, hot ham slices.

Calamondins	Cut off tops and squeeze out juice
1½ cups water **½ cup dark brown sugar** **3 T cornstarch** **¼ t salt** **¼ t allspice** **¼ t cinnamon** **pinch clove**	Cook until syrup is thick and clear.
⅓ cup golden raisins	Add raisins and cook just long enough to heat. Remove from heat and add calamondin juice.

THE SEAGRAPE . . . only those bushes growing by the sea produce good jelly-making grapes. The leaf of the seagrape was used by early Spanish pioneers as stationery for their 16th century letters home.

It still works, Try it some time, using a ball point pen. You can make very original greeting cards.

SEAGRAPE JELLY

Use mostly purple grapes but add a few not-so-ripe ones. Wash in soda water. In twice the amount of water, bring to boil and then simmer until grapes are soft and can be mashed off the seeds with a potato masher. Pour cooked jelly into bag, drain and measure juice so rendered. Measure out an equal amount of sugar, bring juice to boil and add sugar gradually, stirring constantly. Boil vigorously until mixture begins to thicken. Pour into clean, hot jars and process by water bath method.

SURINAM CHERRIES

This is a great doorstep fruit. Shining green leaves and little crimson, pumpkin-shaped fruits make it an attractive ornamental bush. The luscious taste — it's faintly reminiscent of pimiento — is sheer serendipity. Eat them fresh at the doorstep or take them indoors and experiment. When you've had surinam cherry sauce with your turkey you may not want to go back to the common cranberry variety!

SURINAM CHERRY SAUCE

1 cup sugar **½ cup vinegar**	Heat together to dissolve sugar, then cool.
4 cups Surinam Cherries **pits removed.**	Stir into vinegar and chill in refrigerator til needed. (It is better after 2 days).

SURINAM CHERRY JAM

Mix equal parts of pitted surinam cherries and sugar. Cook 30 minutes over low heat or until thickened. Stir to prevent sticking. Pour into sterilized jars and seal.

BANANAS . . . raw or cooked, are consumed by more people than any other fruit in the world. Every village in the tropical worlds of Africa, Asia, or the Americas has its own special favorite. The variety is so great that researchers throw up their hands and say the number is uncountable. However, commercial varieties are few in the Americas because plants selection is limited to those with good "keeping qualities". There is no reason to limit oneself to these varities if a few plants in your back yard is your goal.

Bananas are well suited to backyard culture in Florida. Typically they like lots of water, a sunny spot and a frost-free environment. Soil ph is not critical since they thrive in a ph range of 4.5 to 7.5. They need a high nitrogen fertilizer (such as a lawn fertilizer or manure) and should be protected from the wind. The leaves tear easily which limits fruit production. Since bananas bear fruit in one year, it no great loss even if your Florida plants freeze out during a severe cold spell; new plants spring up as soon as the weather warms up.

Dwarf or Cavendish bananas do particularly well in Florida as they can stand a bit more chilly weather. They are native to tropic highlands where the nights are colder. Their dwarf habit makes them ideal plants for a condominium terrace. They seldom grow taller than 2 meters, yet bear full size fruit.

Bananas are so easily grown and universally liked, it is a wonder why more Floridians don't pick and cook their own fresh fruit.

—Editors

BANANA PINEAPPLE CAKE

2 cups sugar
3 cups flour
1 t. cinnamon
1 t. baking soda
1 t. salt

Sift together

3 eggs, slightly beaten
1½ cups cooking oil
2 cups diced bananas
1 8-oz can crushed pineapple
with juice
10 maraschino cherries. chopped
1 cup nuts

Add to dry ingredients and stir with spoon to mix. (Do not use mixer.)
Bake in a tube pan for 1 hour and 20 minutes at 350 degrees.

BANANA BREAD

The easiest of all banana breads. You don't need to beat the eggs. Nor add ingredients in any particular order. Just toss it all together, stir it to mix, and bake.

2 cups flour
1 cup sugar
½ cup shortening
2 eggs
Juice and grated rind
of 1 orange
4 large bananas, mashed
½ cup black walnuts
1 t. baking soda
½ t. salt

Mix all ingredients and bake in loaf pan for 1 hour at 350 degrees.

JAMBOLAN or JAVA PLUM

Four years from planting a seed, you can pick fruit from a twenty-foot tall Jambolan tree. Not just some fruit, but usually so much you couldn't use it up or give it away. Some people like it fresh but it's best for making fine jelly. This recipe is from "Uncle Pasco" Roberts.

In a heavy pot, put Java Plums and enough water to almost cover them. Cook 30 to 45 minutes until plums break open and turn pink. Crush fruit thoroughly and strain through a cloth, squeezing to obtain juice.

4 cups Java Plum juice
½ cup lemon juice
6½ cups sugar

Bring to a rolling boil.

½ bottle Certo

Add Certo, bring back to boiling point and boil one minute.
Pour into sterilized jars and seal.

INDEX